Elusive Peace
India & Pakistan

Elusive Peace
India & Pakistan

Pushpa Dodani

2006
Kaveri Books
New Delhi - 110 002

First Published in 2006

ISBN 81-7479-078-0

Published by
Rakesh Goel
Kaveri Books
4697/5-21 A, Ansari Road,
New Delhi - 110 002 (India).

Tel.: 011-2 328 8140, 2 324 5799
e-mail: kaveribooks@vsnl.com

Laser Typesetting by
Aarati Computers, Delhi - 110 009.

Printed at
Chawla Offset Printers, Delhi-52.

PRINTED IN INDIA

Dedicated

to the fond memories

of my beloved

Amma, Baba, Daddy
and
Guide Dr. Amita Agarwal

Preface

The history of Indo-Pakistan relations has mainly been a story of conflict and discord, mutual distrust and suspicion. A continuing Seige mentality on both sides, fuelled by bitter historical memories, deep rooted prejudices and undying mistrust, is a powerful political tool for fanning public passions in the hands of those decision makers and governmental institutions having vested interest in perpetuating hostilities. Hard line politicians and policy makers on both sides, denigrate dialogue and promote enemy images, aided in their task of manipulating public opinion by sympathetic segments of the media, and years of indoctrination through state controlled educational systems.

U.S. policy towards South Asia began with a low profile engagement in the regional affairs during the post independent period and obtained a high profile during the cold War years. U.S. policy vis-à-vis South Asia is two pronged, it is directed to encourage an India-Pakistan settlement on the Kashmir dispute and supporting an Islamabad – New Delhi understanding on the nuclear issue. On a broader level the U.S. – South Asian relations are also shaped by growing co-operation in economic and commercial fields, which has become imperative for it in a way to shoulder its duties and obligations successfully towards the world community as the only super power after the disintegration of USSR.

First chapter of the study introduces the subject and gives a general description of the problem to be investigated.

Second chapter analyses South Asia as a region and makes an attempt to study the various tearing forces within the region.

Third chapter discusses the Indo-Pak relations during Clinton Administration with special references to the U.S. policies.

Fourth chapter makes an attempt to study peace prospects in South Asia with special references to US policies towards the region.

Fifth chapter analyses the impact of 9/11 on the international relations specially as it affects the concept of security and it also makes an attempt to require a new thrust between India and Pakistan so that they can come out of fifty eight years of bloody conflicts.

The last, and concluding chapter, as usual, sums up the study and seeks to suggest ways and means to enhance peace in the region.

Dr. Pushpa Dodani

Contents

1

Prologue

South Asia may be called the heart of the underdeveloped world and is a pivotal area in contemporary international relations. It is today one of the world's greatest laboratories of political economic and social change. It embodies all the hopes and most of the problems of human kind.

South Asia, if we include Peoples Republic of China (PRC), has the largest concentration of population in the entire world. It is an area of great geopolitical significance, whether viewed from a regional continental or global standpoint. It is also an area full of distressed people whose living standards are among the lowest in the world. At the moment, there is an apparent political economic and social stability but underneath the surface great pressures are building up and great changes are under way.

The home of ancient civilizations and new nations, South Asia throughout the centuries has had a remarkable degree of geographic and cultural unity and its people have a shared common historical experience, but it has never been united politically or socially. Aside from the great divisions that have separated Aryans from non-Aryans, Hindus from Muslims, caste from caste, region from region, literate from illiterate, village from town people, Hindi speaking from non-Hindi speaking, the peoples of the Subcontinent have been torn between the past and present, and they have often found it difficult to reconcile their objectives with realities. History and nature have been unkind to them[1].

They have developed one of the most stable and meaningful, but also one of the most rigid and stratified of social systems. This social system is proving to be increasingly inadequate under modern conditions, and the people of the Sub continent are facing the unwelcome prospect of inevitable change in unknown directions.

End of Cold War and a New Beginning:

Before taking up the specific issue of peace and security in South Asia, a quick look at the rapidly changing international order is necessary. The developments in early 1990's, especially the liberation war of Kuwait and the disintegration of the Soviet Union, resulted in an uncertaintly in the international system. Majority of the nation states in the world are trying to keep their options open. In this backdrop one can discern six broad trends in the world at present. They are:

i. The post colonial impulse and motivations, which determined foreign policy of most of the developing countries, have come to an end.

ii. The last five decades have transformed developing societies individually and the community of nations collectively. Factors effecting national identities and their territorial security, the nature of development and economic interests and external equations, have undergone a change and are effecting the security policies of all nation states.

iii. Higher levels of political awareness amongst the masses have generated higher levels of political expectations. Therefore economic, social and security concerns of each nation state has undergone a perceptible change.

iv. At a more important level of the political structure of societies, especially in the developing countries, linguistic, ethnic and religious groups are challenging the concept of the nation state itself.

v. While the developing countries are busy with the process of nation building, the developed countries' quest for resources of the globe and their management is on the top of their agenda.

vi. Lastly, the great powers have shown a decisive attitude in withdrawing from some of the troubled spots of the developing countries, like Afghanistan and Cambodia, signaling to the parties involved to sort themselves out.

Security is the ultimate quest for all. It is the universal experience and constant preoccupation of mankind in its individual, social and corporate existence[2]. In the past, security has been viewed in terms of power relations between states or in terms of military defence against external threats. However, it has undergone major changes in recent years. One of the most significant aspect of this change is the increasing importance given to its multi-dimensional implications. Security is no longer viewed as an exclusive domain of military considerations. It now encompasses the entire realm of social, economic, political, military and environmental aspects with a view to attaining comprehensive development. It is the culmination of presence of values, satisfaction of needs, a sense of security, and striving for unhindered growth and development[3]. Thus, in the present day world, security means development and anything detrimental towards attaining this objective is a threat to security as McNamra observes, "Security means development. Security is not military hardware. Though it may involve it, security is not military activity, though it may encompass it. Security is development and without development there can be no security"[4].

The security of South Asia revolves round two variables:

1. South Asia is riven by ethnic and social unrest, beset by intra-regional conflict, swept by nationalism, facing economic ruins, abandoning the substance if not the form of democracy and posing a threat of nuclear proliferation.

2. South Asia may become a bulwork of stability - a well-integrated region with solidified and expanding democratic structures, moving toward a modest prosperity that is more fairly distributed than is now the case at present[5].

A genuine commitment to the principles of UN Charter can provide the basis for the initiation of a comprehensive peace process in the South Asian region. But this effort is not sufficient to enhance the absolute peace in the region, because when two traditional rival powers India and Pakistan engage the attention of the world by entering into a competitive nuclear arms race which has been termed as a race for Mutually Assured Distribution (MAD) a diche' of the Cold War days. The nuclearisation of the Sub-continent has began. It has not gone without building up tension in the region. The world around is watching agape in wonder as to what has set the "Midnights children" so far apart. The self-acclaimed monitors of international peace have stumbled upon Kashmir as the root cause. The end of the Cold War has unleashed several hopes and aspirations as well as concerns and worries not only for Europe and America, but also for the rest of the world. One of the basic problem or challenge that the collapse of the Cold War regime has posed to many regions of the Third World is the problem of national integration, South Asia being a region consisting of multi-ethnic states.

Ethnic resurgence as a concept is of relatively new currency. Not that the idea was non-existent earlier, but it was known under different nomenclatures. Probably there is an inherent logic behind it. While the nationalistic demands by definition should end up achieving independent statehoods, more autonomy within the existing structure is supposed to be the optional solutions.

Although South Asia with its well-defined external boundaries, constitutes a coherent region, its internal political geography follows no clear lines of demarcation. This is to be largely expected in such an ancient crucible of civilization where peoples, cultures and religions are inextricably interwoven. Boundary demarcations invariably cut across communities and tribes. The three major river systems the Indus, the Ganges and the Bramhaputra cut across the boundaries of India, Pakistan, Bangladesh and Nepal and have further exacerbated the tensions between them, resulting in disputes over the share of waters[6].

Moreover, five of the six[7] states in South Asia have borders with India and this has resulted in inevitable complications since all these states are in their infancy, and in several areas the boundaries are not yet firmly settled. India, which looms large as the center-piece, shares ethnic, religious and cultural affinities with all its neighbours. A central and most persistent theme in South Asia has been Indo-Pakistan rivalry. Before departing in 1947, the British had divided their Indian empire into India and Pakistan because it was argued, the warring Hindus and Muslims could not be amicably reconciled to sharing the country. The partition itself was marked by some of the worst carnage in history. Far from ending Hindu-Muslim rivalry it elevated the inter-community bloodbath into inter-state rivalry. India and Pakistan have fought three major wars in 1947, 1965 and 1971, and recently the fourth undeclared war in 1999 but its fate is yet to be resolved.

India has come a long way as a claimant to the regional power status in South Asia taking into account her historical potential as well as international standing. Indian strategists developed a series of well-connected foreign policy and security perceptions with regard to its role in determining the destiny of South Asia, which are widely known as the Indian Doctrine. To a significant extent it is the South Asian version of the "Monroe Doctrine" wherein India views the entire region as a single strategic unit and herself as the sole custodian of security and stability in the region[8].

As the concept of security is multi dimensional and a new dimension can be added at any time, this theory should be flexible enough to accommodate various changes. In the concept of security, National and International security are intertwined in such a manner that it is difficult to differentiate between them. In the present world international security is getting prominence as the bi-polar confliction world is heading towards a multi-polar consensus world. Instead of warfare, peace is acknowledged as a prime mover of nations. The main objective therefore is global peace and all round development of the world[9].

The post-Cold War era is characterized by two distinct and interrelated phenomena. On the positive side, the world has made a decisive shift away from conflict to a course of cooperation. The delicate balance between defence and development has clearly tilted in favour of the latter. On the other hand, the convergence of ideologies and broader interests of the developed countries have brought a virtual end to a crucial balance that existed in international politics. Thus the post-Cold War era has opened up new opportunities for the Third world in terms of resolving some of the outstanding conflicts[10].

Extra regional involvement was invited by the feuding South Asian countries themselves either to face the unchallengeable regional adversary or to neutralize extra regional involvement in favour of a regional antagonist. As a matter of fact, throughout the entire post colonial period, feuding parties in South Asia have almost invariably invited extra-regional great powers in regional conflicts, while the latter with competing interests have made persistent efforts, in one way or the other, to shape a regional balance deemed to serve their broader strategic perceptions. As a consequence extra regional involvement in South Asian conflicts has become a constant phenomenon. In certain cases the momentum of the conflicts was sustained largely due to competitive involvement of the extra regional great powers[11].

During the entire Cold War period the conflict scenario in South Asia was dominated by two antagonists, India and Pakistan. The extra regional great powers were also divided along the same line the US and China on Pakistan's side, and the Soviet Union on India's side. Along with India and Pakistan these three powers, the US, the Soviet Union and China, have been the determinants of regional politics in South Asia with regard to both conflict and cooperation. Conflicts in the region have often been complicated by competitive involvement of extra regional powers. In certain cases however crisis have been defused and wars have been stopped, thanks to Great Power efforts. The "Tashkent Accord" is a case in point. In the past, the Cold War vitiated the atmosphere in the region and gave impetus to conflicts, while relaxation of tensions among the Great Powers created favourable conditions by at least minimizing the external inputs to conflicts in the region. Therefore, it was only natural to expect that the radical changes that took place at the global level, particularly the withdrawal of the competitive involvement of Super and Great Powers from the Third World regional conflicts would create favourable conditions for the settlement of conflicts and enhanceg the emerging process of cooperation in the region. The conflict scenario in South Asia, however remained virtually unaffected by the withdrawal of competitive involvement of extra-regional Great Powers from the region. The primary reason is that it has only removed the external inputs from the conflicts, which have only been partly responsible for their outbreak or sustenance, and never played a decisive role. A complex web of reasons that continue to bedevil security situation in South Asia is rooted within. A genuine commitment can provide the basis for the initiation of a comprehensive peace process in the South Asian region. Incorporating three distinct but correlated sub-processes of a political action aimed at peaceful settlement of disputes, a Disarmament process and Confidence and Security Building Measures. It is important to understand the correlation between these sub-processes. They are complementary processes, which must be initiated simultaneously through an institutionalized forum. Each sub-process makes its own contribution in reducing frictions and lowering tensions and thereby acts as stimulant for the others. Their combined effect generates stability, peace and cooperation. It is therefore essential that progress in all spheres be made simultaneously as deadlock or lack of progression in one is bound to affect the others, and impede the downward momentum. The situation in South Asian region is that whereas creation of CBMs has been agreed upon between India and Pakistan, disarmament has received no serious attention and the core issue of Kashmir remains deadlocked. The value of CBMs in such circumstances will at best be marginal and liable to criticism due to misuse of the process to circumvent more important issues. The process should be institutionalized and periodic discussions on all issues must be held at political and official levels. Assistance of regional or international forums must be sought for resolution of issues over which there is a deadlock in bilateral negotiations over a considerable period of time. A threat and tension free atmosphere is necessary for smooth progress in the political process. This can best be achieved by the establishment of a stable military regime through the institution of a set of Disarmament and Confidence and Security Building Measures.

South Asia and Global Political Trends

South Asia is a more recent construction - only about five decades old -which today encompasses seven diverse sovereign states of very different sizes: three countries that form the Sub-continent: India, Pakistan, and Bangladesh, two island states, Sri Lanka and Maldives and two Himalayan Kingdom Nepals and Bhutan.

South Asia has a vast geographical grace stretching from the Himalayan mountain ranges in the North to the Indian Ocean in the South, and from the valley of the Indus in the West to the plains of the Bramhaputra in the East. This huge geographical expanse has become home to a teeming population, numbering nearly a billion people who account for over a fifth, or to be more precise, 23 per cent of humanity. The Sub-continent carries the weight not only of its people, but also of their ancient history, encompassing the experience of British colonialism compressed in tumultuous development within the past couple of countries centuries.

It is a common place in any introduction to South Asian history to expound on the cliche about the region's unity in diversity. It may be more appropriate to characterize South Asia and its people as presenting a picture of diversity in unity, indeed of immense diversity, within a very broad contour of unity. The geographical boundaries drawn by the highest mountain ranges in the world and encircling seas and oceans set the whole of the Subcontinent apart from the rest of the world. Yet within these boundaries, there is a great diversity in natural attributes - imposing hills and mountains, lush green river plains, arid desert and brown plateaus. People inhabiting such a region, have evolved a shared cultural ambience, but at the same time, are deeply attached to distinctive cultural beliefs and practices.

Ethnicity has been one of the most pervasive features of political life, at national, regional and international levels, during the last half century and more so on it the post Cold War era. Ethnic issues are behind many of the vexing problems and conflicts between and within nations today. The upsurge and intensity of ethno-political strife in recent times have led to the concern that the main threats to international security and stability originate more from ethnic turmoil within nation-states than from other types of conflicts.

The countries of the region are: bound by shared bonds of historical, ethnic, linguistic, cultural and religious nature. People of common ethnic, linguistic and religious identity live in different South Asian states which not only sustain contacts, commonalities and movements of people defying frontiers, but also undermine the process of constructing nations out of states. What started with the ranges of Partition of the subcontinent along religious lines has continued over the years on account of political and economic factors.

The challenge of transforming ethnic and religious diversities into nationhood remains endemic in South Asia, most often exacerbated by the failure of the dominant majority community to provide democratic space to other social groups. The pitfalls and distortions in this transformation process - like discriminatory legislation and flawed distributive justice, account for conflict in the nation building process. As a result the state remains unstable politically while the governments are extremely ill prepared to face challenges of effective governance and development. Despite recent positive development in democratic transformation throughout the region, the process of institualization of democracy and the concept of peace and security continues to suffer recurrent setbacks.

Ethnic conflicts have become a major problem in the politics of South Asia. It has been a major contributing factor leading to the rise of guerrilla warfare and political terrorism within the South Asian countries. According to Martin 0. Heisler -

> ".... Ethnic divergence have been the single most important source of long-term conflict leading to civil wars and insurgence and even to the disintegration of states"[12]

There has been a phenomenal rise in ethnicity-based assertions and movement for political power all over the world during the twentieth century. South Asia is no exception. The emancipation of South Asia from the British rule during 1947-48 opened a new chapter in ethnic politics. It has much to do with the emergence of new states in the post Second World War era and growing awareness of people about their separate identities and economic political exploitation of their rights. According to David Levinson, Editor in Chief of Encyclopedia of World Cultures,

> "For the past several years, ethnic conflict has been the World's most common form of collective violence and a major cause of the steadily increasing refugee problem. Ethnic conflicts are generally defined as a violent conflict between or among groups who differ from each other in terms of culture, religion, physical features or languages. Ethnic conflict often involves more than just conflict between groups; some times there is conflict between groups; some times there is conflict between fractions within each group and often other nations and people become involved e.g. the sufferings of Muslims of Sri Lanka in the Tamil-Sinhala conflict"[13].

According to David Robertson, ethnicity involves the whole socio-political spectrum of national identity, that is why ethnic politics takes its most virulent form in the Third World where territorial boundaries of states owe far more to European Empire - builders than to any ethnic homogeneity. Given the overall strength of national identity and the analogous importance of other basic political issues related to organizing a productive economy, ethnic divisions may be absolutely central to the problems of organizing a working political system[14].

> "..... Ethnicity refers to sometimes rather complex combination of racial, cultural and historical characteristics by which societies are occasionally divided into separate, and probably hostile, political families. Although racial political divisions have always been vital where they exist, it is probably only in the last two or three decades that other forms of ethnic politics have become vital though this is not to say that the actual divisions have not been long established and of personal importance. They are for example, crucial ethnicity problems in Belgium and Canada (mainly language conflicts but with associated religious spits), Britain (historical cultural divisions some times fought around language politics but also with religious connections), remnants of such divisions in Scandinavian countries (mainly language again) to mention just a very small sample"[15].

South Asia is undoubtedly the hub of considerable ethnic strife, including Sri Lankan, Tamils and Sinhalese in Sri Lanka; Assamese and Bodo in north-eastern India; Chakma and other tribal people in Bangladesh; Sikhs in India; Kashmiris, Sindhis, Mohajirs, Baluchis, Siraikis in Pakistan; Muslims and Hindus in India and Burmese and ethnic minorities such as the Karen and Mon in Myanmar. Ethnic disturbance can be called as a destabilizing factor to internal stability in South Asia.

South Asia's multi racial, multilingual and multi religious set-up provides a fertile ground for a conflict between centripetal and centrifugal forces. Scarcity of resources, role of media, rise in political awareness and growing violence created a culture for ethnic movements. The weakness of the nation state system in coping with new challenges is further promoting ethnic feelings in a number of South Asian countries. Given its destructive efficacy ethnicity in South Asia is like a time bomb. If mishandled by the rulers it has the capacity to upset territorial status quo and plunge the region into a perpetual state of insecurity and violence. Among factors that have exacerbated ethnic tensions in South Asia the following appear to be the most important:

1. Imprudent handling of ethnic conflicts by the regimes. Instead of dealing with ethnic problem in a political and accommodative manner, excessive force was and is being used to quell ethnic movements. The examples are the use of force by the Pakistan army to crush the nationalists movement in Baluchistan by the first PPP government of Z.A. Bhutto in Baluchistan from 1973 to 1977, the use of force by the military regime of Gen Zia-Ul-Haq in Sindh during 1983-4 and the launching of 'Operation Clean Up' by Islamabad against the Mohajir Quomi Movement (MQM) in urban Sindh in June 1992. The use of force by the Indian government against separatist groups in the north-eastern provinces, Punjab and Kashmir. In Sri Lanka, attempts made by the Sinhala dominated government to crush separatist Tamil elements led to the outbreak of a body civil war. In Bangladesh, successive governments have used force against the tribal people of Chittagong Hill tracts.
2. Strong arm tactics used by the powerful ethnic group to dominate weak groups.
3. Over centralized political and administrative groups about the preservation of their socio-cultural identity.
4. Intolerant attitude and an element of cultural superiority expressed by one ethnic group against other ethnic groups. According to Shaukat Hassan –

   "the resurgence of ethnicity is primarily due to a loss of confidence in the state system, which is widely perceived to represent the exclusive interest of certain ethnic groups. In addition ideological conceptions and symbols have failed to generate wide appeal because of their exclusive nature.

The general tendency in South Asia today toward centralization and personalization of political authority has only increased the inability of the state structure to accommodate ethnic concerns. What is necessary is decentralization in administration and wide devolution of authority so that all communities can directly share the benefits and burdens of the State."[16]

India is a world in itself. Its one billion people practice all the major religions of the world, consist of all the main racial groups, speak more than seven hundred languages and dialects, follow diverse customs and traditions in respect of marriage, divorce, adoption and inheritance and above all, sport a complicated caste system which baffles the wisdom of the South Asian region. British historian Vincent Smith had once characterized India as a case of unity in diversity. This unity, however was traumatically ruptured in 1947 when together with Independence came the division of the country into two sovereign nations one of which was further subdivided in 1971.

Smith's united India now stands fragmented into three independent states - India, Pakistan and Bangladesh. Mercifully, the post independent India has not experienced any dismemberment. Behind this unity of course there have been political, constitutional and military efforts. Autonomy and secessionist demand, have been raised from time to time, but somehow they have been managed, some times satisfactorily, some times not. But there is a problem and it lies elsewhere. There are three broad categories of ethnic demands, and since each demand has some geographical specificity, they may be studied from the perspective of regionalism as well[17].

In the first category are included all those demands which are located in the border regions and which have at some point of time or the other exhibited strong secessionist impulses. Parts of the north-east and the Kashmir valley fall under this category.

Recently Punjab and decades ago Tamil Nadu have shown similar tendencies.

The second category consists of all those demands which are not secessionist but are in favour of more autonomy which can be possible according to their protagonists in the creation for Uttarakhand in Uttar Pradesh, Jharkhand in Bihar, Gorkhaland in West Bengal, Vidarbha in Maharashtra, Bodoland in Assam etc. are some of the current linguistic terms which had led to the partitioning of Assam, Mumbai, Chennai and Punjab and the creation of several new states.

In the third category are included all those demands which seek more autonomy, preferably within newly carved states in the Indian Union, but are otherwise willing to settle for less, at least for governments to manage their local administrative and developmental affairs. The agitation of the Gorkhas of West Bengal, Bodos of Assam, Jharkhandis of Bihar and tribals of the north-east and other parts of the country fall in this category.

Most of the countries of South Asia have been experiencing separatism in one form or the other for many years or even decades since their independence. Ethnicity as a form of separatism has emerged as a most pervasive feature of political life in some of these countries. It now appears to be quite an enduring phenomenon even in well-functioning democracies and in those countries where certain constitutional safeguards and amendments have been brought about to guarantee ethno-cultural harmony in the body politics. Bangladesh's tribal population of the Chittagong Hill Tracts which constitute less than l percent of the country's total, most of which are Buddhists (some are Christians and Hindus), have been waging a violent insurgency in quest of autonomy for the last two decades. It is still more ironic that Bangladesh, which itself is the outcome of a long-fought-out separatist struggle against Pakistan, has been experiencing armed separatism being waged by its South-Eastern hill people.

Since the late 1970s and early 1980s, the spread of ethnic forces in India (particularly in north eastern states and Punjab) and their attempt to defy territorial status-quo led to the eruption of serious political upheavals. In Pakistan the question of ethnicity was considered contradictory to the Islamic ideology of the country or to the basis of its existence, i.e. the two nation theory. The dismemberment of Pakistan in 1971 and the endemic political instability that the country has been confronting in recent years has been symptomatic of a clash between ethnic forces striving to establish a decentralized political structure and the advocates of an Islamic state with a strong central authority. Pakistan is not a homogeneous state. On the basis of its ethnic divisions and because of the lack of an effective common bond, Pakistan has often been pronounced as an 'unnatural country'. Religion, which became a basis for the creation of Pakistan is called a transient arrangement, a fact proved by the emergence of Bangladesh in December 1971, and constant ethnic tensions in the country particularly in Sindh and in Baluchistan.

The Constitution of Pakistan (1973) is silent on the issue of ethnicity and only mentions this question indirectly. Pakistan is the only country in South Asia, which has witnessed its dismemberment in 1971 on ethnic grounds. And even thirty years after the emergence of Bangladesh the country is vulnerable to secessionist and separatist movements like Jiy-Sindh.

Multi ethnicity is a socio-political phenomenon in most of the countries of the world today and ethnic conflicts appear to have acquired marked intensity in recent decades and are expected to be a major source of internal wars in the twenty first century.

Problems related to ethnicity are common to nearly every country of this region. While dimensions and intensity vary from country to country, Sri Lanka presents us with striking case of conflict between the two main ethnic communities; the Sinhalese who formed 74% of the total population in 1981 (a great majority of them 69.3% -Buddhists) formed the Tamils 12.6% and Indian Tamils 5.6% most of them Hindus 15.5%[18].

The Sri Lankan minority forms a majority in the Northern and Eastern provinces of the island. They are socially and economically in a better position than Tamils of recent Indian origin, the great majority of who are plantation workers. These Indian Tamils enjoyed dominant positions in the public services and professions during the British colonial period and for some time even after the Independence. But they found their position challenged by the Sinhalese in the 1950's particularly after the Sinhalese language was made the only official language of Sri Lanka in 1956. The Indian Tamils for their part have been fighting for their fundamental rights such as citizenship and voting rights since independence which were curtailed by D.S. Senanayake government in 1948 and 1949 through a series of legislations.

As opportunities for public service employment dwindled as a result of economic stagnation in the 1960s and 1970s the communal antagonism between the two communities sharpened. The Sri Lankan Tamil minority complained that they were discriminated against by the Sinhalese in state university education. Therefore, they shifted their earlier demand for autonomy to that of separation. How ever, the Indian Tamils chose to cooperate with the Sinhalese leaders of the UNP to find solution to their problem. So did the Muslim minority groups (7.1%)[19].

The political leadership of post independent Sri Lanka has attempted to resolve the ethnic differences by adopting various methods.

Nepal a mountainous country with an area of fifty four thousand square miles and a population of twenty million, is sandwiched between the two most populous countries of the world with diametrically opposite political and social systems– communist China to the North and democratic India to the South. A country never subjugated by any colonial power Nepal is proud of a glorious history of national independence.

The country has witnessed during the ten years under review six governments with constitutional legitimacy but rising fears of instability, chaos and confusion. There are many factors which play a significant role in democratic Nepal, e.g. social groups especially linguistic, religious, cultural, tribal and regional minority categories in the new constitutional order produced by the movement for the restoration of democracy since 1990. Since the preceding regime, which lasted for about 30 years was authoritarian in nature, only a subdued ethnic feeling was observed within the regional (Tarai) and hill communities. So the open debate that took place during and after the Royal proclamation of national referendum in 1979 for eliciting the opinion to determine the fate of the 'party less' regime led by the old order, could provide us with certain emerging trends of ethnicity in the new democratic Nepal. However, as the former regime cannot become the interface of ethnic politics because of limited freedom granted to the citizens of the country as well as the narrow electoral base of the regime.

Problems of Peace and Security in the Region

The discourses on peace and nation building misses the other dimensions of conflicts in societies. The invisible support to conflicts from outside, the supply and diffusions of small arms, and perpetuation of myths (in building the edifices of hate against people and nations) greatly contribute in keeping the conflicts going. These facts equally hinder the processes of peace[20].

To enhance the peace in Sub-continent, security perceptions were constructed on the new realist parameters of:

1. The sovereign state (based on the West phalian system with its sovereign character).
2. State behaviour (premised on rationality and interest).
3. The international system (essentially anarchic), and
4. Ends of security (the normalcy of interstate conflicts)[21].

South Asian security studies have thus relied excessively on the US/ Western paradigms of International relations theory in term of conceptual dependency, analytical enterprise and the resultant, policy analysis, the post Cold War security discourses have an expanded agenda that accounts for internal security challenges and non-traditional military issues. This focus is also a western endeavour that is now gaining increasing relevance and significance in the South Asian Security discourse. The neo-realist international relations theory has provided the next description of the security paradigm. Macro issues of security were in term of the role of nuclear, nuclear deterrence and nuclear balance, traditional security concerns of conventional warfare, capabilities and escalation strategies. The emergent dimension of security the micro-issues that are essentially non-military in nature. They range from ethnic conflict, social conflicts of race, religion, caste and groups resulting in sectarian violence, refugee crises and other serious social economic, political and environmental crises. Thus, the ambit and scope of South Asian security has to balance both the macro and micro issues of security. In the pluralistic essence, security is a much-contested term with flexible scope[22].

The post-Cold War era and the emerging millennium has a new agenda in the security discourse that essentially emanates from the weak statehood foundations of the Third World. The security problems of South Asia are more focused to the pressures, challenges and threat that are societal, political, sub national, cultural, ethnic, communal, demographic, economic, environmental which corrode the fabric of the South Asian state system more than the compulsion of the military strategic threats. The debate between the security of the state in pure terms of "power" and the western ethnocentric preferences of balance of power is indeed obsolescent vis-à-vis the resilience of the state in terms of societal and political stability and economic discourse[23].

The spectrum of non-military issues is indeed wide and complex in the asymmetrical nature of South Asia. The Indo-centric gravity is the main anchor in the plethora of non-military issues[24].

The geographical domain of India is the main plank for all shared problems in terms of ethnic, communal sectarian disputes, cross border terrorist violence and displacement of people as refugees. Ideological differences between the South Asian states have exacerbated regional divisions that have accentuated the common threats faced by South Asia. The fundamental divide is over nation-building strategies, regional order and cooperation. The state system of the countries in South Asia reveals serious weaknesses in the governance process. While experimentation in democracy has been going on relatively new in Bangladesh, Nepal and Pakistan, it has been in India and Sri Lanka since they attained statehood from colonialism. Democratic governance has received a mixed response in South Asia. While India professes a democratic governance model with a federation characteristic, the other states are either fragile democracies or at best Unitarian systems. The other condition is the persistence of territorial / border disputes, river water sharing disputes, aggravating factors in non-military threats in South Asia. Political issues in non-military threats have resulted from three persistent ailments to the body politic, the failure in governance-democratic and authoritarian, both systems have been unable to deliver the goods expected of them. This phenomenon has resulted in the breakdown of law and order, increasing pace of civic strife abetted by the lack of political accountability and civic audit[25].

The loss of a good governance is reflected in the ability of the South Asian state system to conciliate and resolve secessionist demands. Infact the failure has actually accentuated sport a in militancy in the Kashmiri, Sikh, Baluchi, Bodo, Chakma and Tamil separatist movements

The intricate link between the secessionist movements with the transnational forces of narcotics and arms smuggling networks, the links between the regional networks and the international mafia, terrorist, narcotics groups are quite obvious. The inability of the South Asian states to combat these forces is reflected in the powerful impact the groups have on the vulnerabilities of the South Asian states, and the failure of governance adds to the situation. Lack of appropriate responses in policing the porous borders and the lack of regional consensus have been other reasons for the failure of the state.

Another intricate problem has been the dependence of the secessionist groups on external support for resources and material support logistic. Quite often the secessionist groups have found safe havens and bases in the neighbouring states, be it Kashmir, Sikh, Baluchi, Bodo, Chakma or Tamil groups. Terrorism and militancy across the borders have been abetted as low intensity conflicts by the contending states, thus weakening the internal order and civic stability of the states.

Human Rights have legitimate space within the framework of the sovereign nation state. Extrapolating them to a separatist secessionist agenda has diluted their virtue. In conflicts human rights have often been used in opportunistic manner. Kashmiri, Sikh and Tamil secessionism have gained international recognition exploiting these issues. The linkage between Human Rights and Terrorist Militancy is quite precarious.

The political issue as a non-military threat and the social and cultural threats to security: The social cohesion and cultural pluralism of South Asia has come under attack from the proliferation of fundamentalist ideologies, be they be the extreme radicalism of the Maoists or the sectarian doses of religious fundamentalism. These irredentist challenges have emerged as apparent "panacea" to the shortfalls in social economic development[26].

Quite often social economic deprivations and stagnation have been the cause of these irredentist tendencies. Islamization in Pakistan, Hindutva in India, Islamic fundamentalism in Bangladesh and the current vagaries of the social situation in South Asia, the politics of religious majoritarianism vs. minorities is the game being played now. The social cultural agendas of these irredentist claims are the promotion of a 'nationalistic' agenda on the plank of religious nationalism, and the intolerance of other minorities. Nuclear politics in South

Asia has its social cultural stamp of being nationalistic, self reliant and xenophobic.

The spectrum of non-military threats emanating from these political crises poses vital challenges to South Asian security. Securities as construed in these constructs do not have any traditional military responses. The crises of Governance, the culture of political violence are the vital issues in the nonmilitary challenges to South Asian Security. In the prospect the assault is on the fragile foundations of the state and the civil society in South Asia. Bad governance is further abetted by the growing criminalization of politics and the rampant corruption of the politicians and the bureaucrats.

Energy security in South Asia is a significant issue in non-military security. South Asian energy consumption would increase three times by the turn of this century. Besides, with the lack of significant find of hydrocarbons deposits South Asian dependence on imported energy resources would burgeon. A new effort to locate and tap oil and natural gas in the South Asian region has been limited with exception of new finds near Bangladesh. Besides, efforts to access oil from Central Asia from Turkmenistan and Kazakhstan have been stalled due to problems in oil-pipelines being laid in hostile territory[27]. Disruption or hindrance to steady energy flow is yet another non-military challenge that does not have a credible response.

Demographic pressures are emerging to be South Asia's critical non-military challenge. The fast growth of population and pressures on land and resources are big challenges. A serious challenge is the deprivation of the growing urban populace of its due share of resources and the attendant civic strife that would generate.

South Asia state borders are porous, rendering cross borders spillage of population easier either, as economic migrants or as political economic refugees, and in some cases as environmental refugees who have been forced out of their land habitats due to scarcities and environmental calamities[28].

Origins of Conflicts in South Asia: An Overview

	India	Pakistan	United States	Bangladesh, Nepal, Sri Lanka
Major source of conflict	Outsiders upsetting natural Indian dominance	Indian hegemonic ambitions	Regional poverty; unstable region threatens rest of world	Indian domination; arrogance
Secondary source of conflict	Unrepresentative states or leadership, e.g. Pakistani military dictatorship, Nepali monarchy, Sri Lankan and Sinhala elites	Failure of outside Powers to support Pakistan against India	(Formerly) external communist threat against region	Ethnic, environmental and economic pressures
Self-image	Equivalent to 'region' of South Asia	'Homeland', then frontier, for Islam, Then pure Islamic State and people	Benevolent, well-intentioned outsider	Benign and neutral
Image of India-Pakistan Conflict	May last a long time, but India will prevail	Pakistan serves larger regional priority by countering Indian threat	Fundamentally wrong: highest priority should be development; now threatening wider spread of nuclear weapons, etc.	Bangladesh and Nepal: risks regional conflagration Sri Lanka: may be useful to divert India from south

Role of outside Powers	Their misguided meddling only defers the day of regional normalisation	To be drawn into regional struggle against India, as Delhi may threaten their interests	Establish barrier to the spread of regional conflict; and encourage regional cooperation	Primarily for aid and assistance; great risk of annoying India with an alliance
Approach to regional conflict resolution	Bilateral and covert pressure to force the other side to dialogue, or cessation of disruptive activity	Multilateral, extra-regional Powers helpful in ensuring containment of India	Send delegations, threaten to cut aid, avoid direct involvement in regional quarrels	Multilateral and regional

Demographic pressures are directly proportional to the prevalent economic crises and environmental degradation. Illegal migration from Bangladesh to India has been due to economic deprivation and environmental disasters, while those from Sri Lanka have been due to the political situation prevalent there. Quite often demographic shifts in South Asia are attributed acrimoniously as the induction of "Islamic influx" into India.

In the analysis it is evident that the state system in South Asia has been subject to enormous pressures and corrosion from within, the plethora of non-military threats and their vicious links with one another has been responsible for the collapse of the domestic order. In essence, human security in the state has been eclipsed by regime security, individual, minority and the sporadic patterns of violence and criminalization have wrecked the fragile foundations of state in South Asia.

In cumulative assessment a weakened state system, the collapse of law and order, economic stagnation has serious ramifications on the conventional-nuclear balance of the region. Internal disorders and civil strife would essentially weaken the state security apparatus response to external threats. On the other hand, protracted struggle between the security forces and the externally inspired insurgency and terrorism could lead to "hot pursuit" by the defending conventional forces.

References:

1. For a penetrating but controversial analysis of Indian civilization, which stresses the lack of a sense of history, See Riencout de Armaury, the Soul of India (New York: Harper 1960) esp. p.p. 15-16. For a different interpretation See Seminar (New Delhi) No. 39 November 1962 containing a symposium on "Past and Present" esp. articles by Thapar, Romila, Majumdar R.C., Panikkar N.K and Gopal S.
2. Hafiz Abdul M and Khan Rob Abdur (eds.) "Introductory Comments, Security of Small States", University Press United Dhaka 1987, P. 8.
3. Ibid.

4. M.C. Namra, Robert. "The Essay of Security", Harper and Row, New York 1968 P. 146 in Hafiz Abdul M "New Challenges to Security Studies" BIISS Journal Vol. 11 No, 4, 1990.
5. Occasional paper prepared at the time of introducing course paper on South Asia, in the Dept. of Political-Science. JMI 1990.
6. Farmer, H.B. "An Introduction to South Asia", Methuen London 1983 Ch. 1.
7. The Maldives is the seventh state in the South Asian Association for Regional Cooperation (SAARC) but because of the its geographical remoteness from the Sub-continent is not included in the analysis.
8. Sebur Abdur M.K.A. "South Asian Security in the Post Cold War Era".
9. Mishra Amarendra, "Problems in Security: "Quest for a New Theoretical Paradigm" Journal of Peace Studies Vo. IV Issue 21 March-April 1997.
10. Sabur Abdur M.K.A. "South Asian Security in the Post Cold War Era: Issues and Outlook".
11. Ibid
12. Heisler O. Martin, "Ethnic Conflict in the World Today: An Introduction", Annals of the American Academy of Political and Social Science, Vol. 433, 1997. P.1.
13. Levinson David, "Ethnic Conflict and Refugees: The New International Order". Karachi: 12 November 1993.
14. Robertson David. "A Dictionary of Modern Politics". London 1985. P.P. 111-112.
15. Ibid.
16. Hassan Shaukat, Problems of Internal Stability in South Asia PSIS Occasional Papers, Geneva, June 1988 P.54.
17. Regionalism in Indian politics has a varied connotation. It can mean an area consisting of one state, part of a state, parts of more than one state and so on. For a brief explanation of the point, see Chaule K.S. Nationalism and Regionalism in Northeast India: The Pan-Indian context in Deka M.K. (ed.). Nationalism and Regionalism in Northeast India, Dibrugarh 1985, pp. 53-66.
18. Central Bank of Ceylon, Economic and Social Statistics of Sri Lanka. Kelaniya 1981, P. 12.
19. Phadnis Urmila, Ethnicity and Nation Building in South Asia, New Delhi, 1989, p. 13.

20. From Editors desk Journal of Peace Studies Vol. IV Issue 22, May-June 1997, PP. 1.
21. Abraham Itty, "Towards Reflexive South Asian Security Studies" in Wein G. Marvin, South Asia Approaches the Millennium: Re-examining National Security Boulder Westview Press 1995.
22. Buzan Barry, "People States and Feat: An Agenda for International Security Studies in the Post Cold War Era (2nd ed.) Boulder Cob Lynne Rienner 1991.
23. Dally Simon, "Security Modernity, Ecology: The Diemmas of post-Cold War Security Discourses", Alternatives (17) 1992, p. 121.
24. Bajpai Kanti and Cohen Stephen: "Cooperative Security and South Asian Insecurity" in Nolan Jane (ed.) Global Engagement Cooperative and Security in the 21st Century Washington P.C. The Brooking Institution Press 1994 P. 463.
25. Chari R.P. "Newer Sources of Insecurity: The Crises of Government in India", RCSS Policy Papers # 3, Colombo, Regional Centre for strategic studies 1998 PP 5-7.
26. Gupta Shekhar "India Redefines its Role" Adelphi Paper # 293, London International Institute of Strategic Studies 1995, P.20.
27. Kemp Geoffrey and Harkavy Robert, "Strategic Geography and Changing the Middle East" Washington D.C. The Brookings Institution Press 1997, P. 377.
28. Subramanian S.K. The National Security: Scenario Some Issues and Approaches: Indian Defence Review Vol. 11(2) April-June 1996, P. 41.

2

South Asian Spectrum with Special Reference to Indo-Pak Relations

The real bone of contention between India and Pakistan is however Kashmir, which by a process of "accession", belongs to the Indian Union, and yet which Pakistan considers to be a matter of principles "on which its rulers are not prepared to compromise". They have openly said more than once that, "there will be no change in its (Pakistan) stand on Kashmir. When the word P-A-K-I-S-T-A-N was coined, by Chaudhary Rahmat Ali, the letter "P" stood for the Punjab and "K" for the Kashmir; still though the names of those provinces when this sentiment found ample support - notably Sind, Baluchistan and Frontier Province, no where figure in it, though later they became constituents of Pakistan.[1]

Geographically, the state of Jammu and Kashmir can be divided into four segments. First the sub-mountainous and semi- mountainous plain commonly known as Kandi belt, the second, hills including Siwalik Ranges, the third mountains of Kashmir Valley and Sir Punjab Range and fourth the tract of Ladakh, Kargil, Gilgit and Skardu. The state is situated between $30^{0}17^{1}$ and $36^{0}58^{1}$ North latitude and $72^{0}26^{1}$ and $83^{0}30^{1}$ East longitude. Its boundaries extend to Russian Turkistan in North, Tibet in East, Punjab in South and Pakistan in West.

Kalhana, a Kashmiri Pandit who wrote Rajtarangini (the River of Kings) roundabout 1149 A.D, and which undoubtedly is a monumental work in the field of Sanskrit literature, with its lucid and superb style, which can easily be judged from the following lines about Kashmir:

Such is Kashmir, the country which may be conquered but not by armed force where there are hot baths in winter, comfortably landing place on the river banks, where the rivers being free from aquatic animals are without peril, where realizing that the land created by his father is unable to bear heat the hot ranged sun honours it by bearing himself with softness even in summer. Learning high dwelling house, saffron iced water, grapes and the like-what is a common peace there is difficult to secure in Paradise"[2].

"Kashmir", wrote Kalhan, "can be conquered by the powerful spiritual merit but never by the force of soldiers".

The two wings of Pakistan, East and West, separated from each other by about a thousand miles, were as much a part of India by virtue of the British conquests, during 1751-1857, and this vast geographical expanse was held together and administrated from a single dominant centre under a system of unitary government till 1947 when power was transferred by an of Act of British Parliament to two different Dominion governments. The last phase of this fairly long span of unitary government was rendered particularly painful by the policy of "conciliation and counterpoise" on the part of the alien rulers, the end of a liberal tradition, the emergence of extremist forces, the interpolation of religion into politics, the genesis of a two-nation theory, frequent riots between the two leading communities, a growing rift in the Hindu society leading to the identification of "scheduled" castes, and last but not least, an inordinate hurry among the leaders to be in the seats of power at any cost.

The State of Jammu and Kashmir

On quitting India, the British Government gave freedom to the Indian states to accede to India or to Pakistan or to set up as sovereign independent states. By 15th August 1947, all except three states having geographical contiguity with India, had acceded to India on the three subjects of Defence, External Affairs and Communications. The three states, which had not acceded to India were Junagarh, Hyderabad and Kashmir. The ruler of Kashmir offered to enter into standstill agreements with both the countries. Pakistan signed such an agreement but India did not show much anxiety to do so. India had announced that it would enter into standstill agreements only with those states, which had signed the Instrument of Accession. Kashmir had not acceded to India, so there could be no standstill agreement with it. Then circumstances too strong for the ruler of Kashmir, compelled him to accede to India.

On 22nd October, 1947 tribesmen who were assisted by soldiers and officers of the Pakistan army invaded Kashmir. On 24th October the Maharaja felt quite helpless and requested the Government of India for help against this naked aggression. On 26th October he requested the Governor General of India to accept the accession of his state to India. This request was supported by the leaders of the National Conference, then present in Delhi. Lord Mountbatten, the Governor General of India, accepted the accession of the state, but said that the accession would be finally settled after a reference to the people of Jammu and Kashmir. Thus Kashmir became, legally a part of India in the same way as the five hundred and fifty odd other native states had become viz. through their rulers signing an Instrument of Accession and its acceptance by the Government of India[4].

The roots of the Indo-Pakistan conflict are deep. It is possible the two neighbours could have evolved a modus vivendi, and learnt to live in peace and even to build bridges through collaboration in overcoming problems common to both. Events however turned out otherwise.

Two facts about Pakistan must be borne in mind which glaringly stand out in contradistinction with India. The first fact is that after the death of its founder and the assassination of its first Prime Minister, Pakistan has almost all along pursued the line of being a military dictatorship, and of late of a theocracy under the banner of Islam, as against India which by affirmation and to a large extent by practice, is a secular democracy. There could have been a relief from this tradition and Pakistan could have enjoyed an interlude of popular government when Z.A. Bhutto was elected with an overwhelming popular mandate, but this was not to be, because like all his successors, he had no soft corner for India. He went to the extent of declaring that he would wage a 1000 year war against India. Poor Man[1] what to speak of waging a 1000 year war against India, he was not even allowed to run the normal span of his life. And second, in his attitude towards the other regions of Pakistan, say Baluchistan, but specially towards its Eastern wing, Bhutto was out and out an imperialist militarist. He valued his own victory at the polls, but he was not ready to concede it to Sheikh Mujib who had demonstrated a similar feat in his own part of country. Looking back on the whole course of life of this unfortunate man, Bhutto was fond of glamour and was trying to build up a charisma around his personality without being a statesman with a long vision. In his last testament smuggled out of the death cell and printed in India, Bhutto writes:

> "If India had suffered from martial laws and military dictatorship, India would have been in three or four separate pieces by this day. India is more heterogeneous than Pakistan, but India has been kept in one piece by the noise and chaos of her democracy" Wise man! If you knew it so well, why did you let the Eastern wing separate?

The second glaring fact about Pakistan is that whereas India has all along professed, and by and large practised, non-alignment, Pakistan has been aligned with SEATO and CENTO from their very genesis, and Pakistan's allegiance to the American global diplomacy has been further facilitated by the persistent military dictatorship in that country. Military dictators owe no accountability to the people and are free to make themselves tools in the hands of foreign powers. Or to put it in a slightly different way seated on power, military dictators become most susceptible to corruption and when the massive aid in money is added with substantial aid in arms and ammunitions, dictators welcome it as the most visible support for their dictatorial regime. The most sinister thing has happened not so much from countries, which are avowedly totalitarian but from countries, which are proud of their faith in democracy. For when it comes to a global strategy, the same rulers of a so-called democratic country do not entertain even an iota of hesitation to extend support to a dictatorial regime in another country against another democracy[4].

Thus the crux of the Indo-Pak dispute is not to be found in the canal water dispute nor in trade and transport link, shipping protocol or postal agreements. These in themselves would never have been big hurdles in the way of the establishment of peace between the two countries. The real big hurdle is Kashmir, which with Pakistan is a matter of "principle" and as long as this remains intact and alive, no peace is worth the ink it is written with. In this matter of "principle" Pakistan always tries to disturb the atmosphere of India by various types of operations. For instance "Operation Gibrattar" and "Operation Topac" and its recent aggression in Kargil.

The more India talks before the world about Pakistan's interference, more the denials from Pakistan. The Indian Presidents, Prime Ministers and Foreign Ministers have, in many international fora, given details of the assistance being provided by Pakistan to Kashmiri militants, Besides this, the question of Pakistan interference in Kashmir and Punjab figured during several talks at the Foreign Secretary and Defence Secretary level between India and Pakistan. But Pakistan expressed its helplessness in understanding the language of India. It is perhaps due to the fact that Indian rulers have not learnt to use the language that the rulers of Pakistan understand. Pakistan is taking advantage of this weakness of India and continues to formulate its strategy for a proxy war.

India continues to delay in understanding Pakistan's plans and conspiracies which is clear from an announcement of Pakistani President Ghulam Ishaq Khan who had said that, "Pakistan is incomplete without Kashmir". India's laziness in giving a befitting reply is the biggest success of Pakistan and a major encouragement for its continued interference. It is because of this that repeated warnings of serious consequences from India are thrown in waste paper basket by the Pakistani rulers who keep on increasing their interference. What can be moreridiculous than this that Pakistan on our soil, is encouraging our youth (misguided) in battling against our own troops for completing its unfinished task which it could not complete through direct wars.

In the context of the international situation Pakistan has realized that it cannot succeed in grabbing Kashmir either by undeclared or declared war. In the light of geographical and military position of India, Pakistan had realized that in the heat of war against a country of the size of India the existence of Pakistan can be in danger. Therefore it has changed its war strategy.

The background of this new war strategy was Pakistan's fifty years of experience, and especially its rejection of the advice the Chinese Premier Chou-En-Lai, had given during the 1965 war against India. At the time, the then Pakistan Foreign Minister, Z.A. Bhutto had, after prolonged consultations with Army Commanders formulated the plan for "Operation Gibraltar".

As per this "operation" Pakistan attempted to infiltrate thousands of its troops from the so called Azad Kashmir route into the Indian border villages. Its aim was that at the time of Pakistani invasion these infiltrators would terrorise the local people and guide the Pakistani troops. The Chinese Prime Minister Chou-En-Lai had given vital information to Pakistan in order to make some amendments in the "Operation". The obstinacy and excitement on the part of the Army officers did not enable them to render the suggestions. The "Operation Gibraltar" was started but Pakistan had to face defeat because of the courage, bravery and wisdom of the Indian soldiers. At that time the seeds of separatism had been sown in Kashmir but they had not yet sprouted. The inclination and the mind that were needed for making the "Operation Gibralter" a success were missing among the Kashmiri youth. The base on which the "Operation Gibralter" had been started was not strong. The Indian Army officers shattered the dreams of Pakistan.

Then Pakistan launched the proxy war in the name of "Operation Topac". The entire scheme was formulated by former military dictator of Pakistan, Gen. Zia-Ul-Haq. According to well known journalist Altaf Gowhar, Pakistan's proxy war is an amended version Operation Gibralter" and is based on the suggestions of Chou-En-Lai and was named of "Operation Topac". The "Operation" type prolonged campaign used to be carried out during the hey day of imperialism. The Soviet Union had adopted a similar plan in Mongolia, Yugoslavia, Czechoslovakia and Hungary, where attempts had been made to convert the youth to communism. The "Operation" was the result of these experiences and war strategies.

The "Operation Topac" had four main aims -

i) Giving training to Kashmiri youth in the handling of sophisticated weapons.

ii) To destabilise and discourage state administration.

iii) To make the Kashmir Valley a Hinduless area.

iv) To prepare Kashmiri Muslims for "Jehad".

The above mentioned facts clearly indicate that Pakistan had launched a proxy war against India in Kashmir which had been carried out successfully on the shoulders of Kashmiri youth. It is that form of war, which is being fought on our soil, with our money and against our people. Pakistan has not staked anything but we have staked everything.

In this background, the Pakistani claim over Kashmir holds no water, whereas the one-third of Kashmir, which Pakistan holds should be returned to India. Kashmir dispute does not exist between India and Pakistan rather, it has been raked by Pakistani leaders. They have intervened in India's internal affairs and they have also exploited the Muslim sentiments across the border where eleven crores Muslims, a larger chunk of total world Muslim population, are living with dignity and in freedom of professing and preaching Islamic principles which recognize the universal brotherhood. Pakistan has been demanding plebiscite in Kashmir, so that people could exercise their right to live with any of the two countries. Kashmir has been given special status under Article 370 of Indian Constitution. It has been permitted to maintain the independence and distinct identity of Kashmir and its culture, within the larger framework of Indian culture.

The Simla Agreement signed between the two countries in 1972 was an attempt to provide a framework for resolving the Kashmir issue. Simla Agreement seeks to restrain both parties for resorting to internationalisation of dispute, as it is a bilateral problem between the two countries which should not involve third party and the role of UN under this agreement was Minimised More worried about 90000 POWs captured by India, Z.A. Bhutto signed Simla Agreement so that POWs could be returned to Pakistan.

The experience of more than five decades convinced the strategists of Pakistan about the futility of full-scale military adventures in Jammu and Kashmir. In this process, the real issue of vacating the part occupied by Pakistan was relegated to the background and a term "Kashmir dispute" was coined to misguide the world public opinion. The launching of aggressions in violation of agreements and manipulating the international public opinion on Kashmir is the continuum of Pakistan's strategy on Kashmir.

In this regard, this problem did not only strain relations between India and Pakistan, but also affected the Indo-US relations due to US's strategic interest in Kashmir, which borders the Soviet Union, China and Afghanistan. Additionally, the US had a strategic interest in Pakistan as the linchpin of the so-called "Northern Tier"[5].

Though on the whole, the US initially considered India's adoption of policy of non-alignment immoral, but with time, its attitude towards India on this basis seems to have undergone some changes. This conclusion can well be comprehended by analyzing the US reactions to regional conflicts, which were of crucial importance to India, like the Kashmir problem and Kargil war.

Ever since the Kashmir problem was tabled in the UN, the US has been involved in it. However, the US view of this can only be comprehended from the perspective of the Cold War and US attempts at containing international communism. Actually, the main concern and interest of the US at the end of British colonial system in India, was to prevent the problem from escalating into a general war between the two countries as this would adversely affect US policies and strategies in Asia generally, and might push either or both of the belligerents into the communist camp[6].

Coincidentally, the Kashmir problem emerged at the peak of communist "expansionism". Hence, the US predicament was based on the fragility of the general situation and this was further accentuated by the Indo-Pakistan war of 1965[7].

The US considered the origin of the problem to be complex, enmeshed deeply as it was in historical, emotional and political factors and for it, the fundamental task was the disposition of the problem. Thus, the US welcomed the Indian and Pakistani acceptance of the resolution of the United Nations Committee on India and Pakistan (UNCIP) of August 13, 1948 and January 5, 1949. The US felt that this formed the basis of a political compromise in providing for a plebiscite on the future of Kashmir. This was supplementary to both the ceasefire and the truce arrangements. The plebiscite was to be held so that the population of Kashmir could choose without coercion and intimidation from the military forces of either country. Again the US stressed an enduring settlement based on de-militarisation, a ceasefire and a plebiscite. In general, the desire of the US was to bridge the gap between the views of the belligerents so as to reduce the incentive for was. The principles by which the US hoped to achieve this objective wag enumerated by Earnest A. Gross, US representative in General Assembly[8].

Most importantly, the US believed that plebiscite would be the final step in resolving the problem. Therefore, apart from stressing the "fair and impartial" nature of the plebiscite under UN auspices, the US also argued that the interests of both sides would be protected by a fair plebiscite.

Overall, the US concern in this problem has been with a settlement, which would allow both India and Pakistan to work together in defending the regional disputes. The Strobe Talbott - Jaswant Singh dialogue throws light on the US priorities in the South Asian Subcontinent The US is prepared to continue to use its good offices with India and Pakistan to try to foster or encourage direct dialogue between the two countries on the key issues that divide them and have been the source of such enmity and occasional conflict over the years, that of course includes the issue of Kashmir[9].

The fourth war of Kashmir: Kargil

While perfidy, 'backstabbing', 'breach of trust' and many other such expressions have been used to describe Pakistani intrusions in Kargil, the fact remains that Kargil did catch the Government of India napping. While the entire country led by A.B. Vajpayee was raising toasts to the success of his bus journey to Lahore and the consequent Lahore Declaration, Pakistan was engaged in dispatching its troops to the icy heights of Kargil. Irony is that it was not the first time that we have been caught unawares. Pakistan's first three wars had failed to achieve its central objective of acquiring Jammu and Kashmir. The first war was started on October 20, 1947 with irregulars led and supported by the Pakistani Army. The second war started on August 6, 1965. With the launching of the 6000, strong "Force Gibraltar" followed by a full scale invasion, "Grand Slam", led by its armoured divisions. The third war was more difficult, with regular military forces employed in what may be termed as the first phase in the battle for the Siachen area after prolonged preparations to create legitimacy. Failing in this phase Pakistan started intruding in the sub-border districts of

Indian Punjab since 1984 to prepare the ground for subsequent action. This started in July 1988 in the state of Jammu and Kashmir, while militancy in the northwestern portion of Punjab was concurrently stepped up. Barring the battle for Siachen the third war had been prosecuted by Pakistan at the sub-conventional level using its extensive expertise and huge stocks of weaponry built up during its own proxy war against Afghanistan since 1973, and more extensive war against the Soviet forces after 1981, when it became the "front line state" for the United States against its Cold War enemy. The fourth war conducted in Drass-Kargil Batalik sectors of Ladakh witnessed a modified approach, which draws heavily from its experience in prosecuting the Taliban-Pakistan Army joint force operations against the legitimate government in Kabul, to the traditional goals of Pakistan.

As per the recent statement of Dr. Samar Mubarakmand, who supervised the nuclear tests in May 1988, Pakistan manufactured a nuclear device and tested it in 1983[10].

From then on Pakistan's undermining its commitment to the Simla Agreement in various ways is history. What was important was the acquisition of nuclear weapons by 1987, followed by the armed violence initiated in Kashmir since July 31, 1988. The statement of General Aslam Beg, as Army Chief a year later, proclaiming that Pakistan had a new strategy to take Kashmir under its doctrine of "offensive defence", which would result in war being fought on Indian territory, was revealing.

Pakistan appears to have curiously adopted a near similar set of assumptions for its fourth war as it had done in the earlier wars and with similar results of their turning out to be flawed to the degree that the ignominy of defeat was intensified and consequently bitterness aggravated. Pakistan's assumptions on which it constructed its invasion, may be outlined as follows:

1. Nuclear "umbrella" allows offensive action without risks.
2. International community would intervene or stop the war at an early stage.

3. Because of its tension with India since May 1998, China will adopt a stance favourable to Pakistan, if not actually provide strong support.
4. The coalition government in India, weak and undecisive will either over react or under-react.
5. India is militarily weak and unprepared.
6. Indian frustration will lead to escalation putting the onus for escalation on India.
7. Establish a military bridgehead across the LOC. Cut and occupy the Zojila Pass-Leh road. This would seriously effect logistics of the Indian Army in the Ladakh region (including the Siachen sector), which could be further exploited.
8. Attack along the Shyok Valley to gain control of the southern flank of the Siachen-Nubra area.
9. Waves of Taliban / Mujahideen would go through the Pakistani positions on the dominating heights of the Drass-Kargil Batalik sector to flood the Ladakh region and infiltrate into Kashmir from the northern flank. India then would not be able to hold on to Siachen and Ladakh and Kashmir Valley would soon follow.
10. At the minimum, the operation under the garb of Mujahideen would focus attention on Kashmir and Pakistan would be able to claim this as a victory[11].

One of the key assumptions of Pakistan in launching its offensive has been the nuclear factor. It gives the Pakistani establishment a sense of confidence that India will not be in a position to send its forces across the border in a retaliatory strike.

By sending heavily armed foreign mercanaries and army soldiers in civilian clothes across the LOC, Pakistan has added a new dimension to its ten year old "Proxy War" against India. Pakistan's provocative action has compelled India to launch a firm but measured and restrained military operation to clear the intruders. Operation "Vijay" finely calibrated to limit military action to the Indian side of the LOC, includes air strikes from fighter-ground attack (FGA) aircraft and attack helicopters. Even as the Army and the Indian Air Force employ their synergised combat potential to eliminate the intruders and regain the territory occupied by them, the government is keeping all channels of communication open and is willing to negotiate at the diplomatic and political levels with Pakistan to ensure that the intrusions in Kargil are vacated and Pakistan's military adventurism is not allowed to escalate into a larger conflict.

What is the underlying cause behind this strategic blunder? Clearly, the Pakistani military establishment was becoming increasingly frustrated with India's success in containing militancy in Jammu and Kashmir within manageable limits, saw in the Kashmiri peoples open expression of their preference for returning to normal life, the evaporation of all their hopes and desires to bleed India through a strategy of "a thousand cuts".

Pakistan's basic strategy for the fourth war for Kashmir was to position an armed force across the well established formally accepted LOC in the Kargil sector in Jammu and Kashmir in the form of a bridgehead during the winter months, which could be expanded as the season changed. The area selected was along the northern axis covering the Indus and Shyok River Valley. A crucial component of the strategy was the domination of the Drass Kargil road, which provides the only road link between Srinagar in Kashmir and Leh in Ladakh. There have been reports that Pakistan's plans for such an operation to cut the Indian supply lines to Siachen and thereafter move the Pakistan Army in the north to take Siachen region have existed at least since 1994[12].

Other reports from Washington indicate that planning for the invasion had been initiated at least two years earlier[13].

Former Pakistani Army Chief Mirza Aslam Beg also confirmed that with the occupation of the Kargil Drass heights, "Indian troops in Siachen Leh and beyond have been placed in a difficult position"[14]. Beg argued for sustained military pressures on India to force it to negotiate on Siachen and Leh as the first step toward the solution of the Kashmir problem. This objective is possible and can be achieved within a period of six to eight months[15].

The basic concept of the strategy as evident in the battle for Siachen had been evolved a long time before this year. In fact, Altaf Gauhar who was the influential information adviser to Field Marshal Mohammad Ayub Khan has now stated that there was certainly an operational plan by 1987, which was almost put into action. Quoting here would be appropriate:

"The occupation of the strategic hilltops in Drass Kargil and Leh has been a major objective of the Pakistan ever since the Indians occupied Siachen.... In 1987, General Zia-ul-Haq authorised the preparation of a war plan to occupy several positions in the Kargil sector. Sahibazada Yaqub Khan, who was Foreign Minister at the time, was invited to the final meeting of the War Committee in which General Zia was to approve the plan. Sahibzada Yaqub saw the plan, which had not been discussed with him earlier. He said that he was holding the Foreign Affairs portfolio but he had been an army officer all his life and would like to express his opinion about the military appropriateness of the plan. The posts, which Pakistani soldiers would occupy were totally covered by snow almost throughout the year. It was extremely difficult to maintain communications with the posts and meet the day-to-day requirements of the soldiers, who had earlier occupied a similar post and been killed. Their dead bodies were still to be recovered. He added that as Foreign Minister, he would find it difficult to justify Pakistan's military action. General Zia was so impressed with this presentation that he dropped the plan"[16].

This prudence could not last long and the plan was given life in 1994[17]. At this time some reports were published quoting unnamed US official sources, that planning for the Kargil operation had begun at least two years ago[18]. According to a senior commander of the Tehrike-Jihad, Zulquaranian, preliminary exercise for this operation had started by the winter of 1997[19].

It is now fairly clear that the initial elements of Pakistan's firm planning for the war started some time in the winter of 1997 based on earlier plans, which were now dusted and taken out. As a leading Pakistani newspaper put it, "Kargil operation was put on the drawing board by competent military minds many years ago. Kargil was presented as a 'do-able' option when the time was ripe, partly as military revenge for the loss of Siachen and partly as a political device to spur the Kashmiri mujahideen towards greater sacrifice and heroism[20].

The United States has always valued Pakistan as a useful ally in its global Cold War strategy as well as a conduit to the Middle East. Hence, it had a tendency to lean toward Pakistan rather than India on Kashmir. During the Cold War the US also turned a blind eye towards Pakistan's nuclear programme. Even after the end of the Cold War when Congress mandated sanctions could no longer be avoided both in the early 1990s and in 1993, the United States watered down the sanctions in order to prop up a sagging Pakistan.

Role of the US during the Kargil crisis evoked considerable public attention. It was hailed as a realistic assessment of the situation. It was also viewed as a paradigm shift in the US policy toward South Asia.

There is no denying the fact that Washington exerted diplomatic pressure on Pakistan right form the start of the Kargil crisis both at the bilateral and multilateral levels. President Clinton's telephonic admonitions to Nawaz Sharif, the G-8 communiqué on the visit of General Zini, commander in chief of the US Central Command and the raising of the issue at the South Asia Task Force meeting in the Kiev were reflective of this effort. It culminated in the visit of Nawaz Sharif to Washington and his promise to ensure the withdrawal of all Pakistani and Pakistan supported forces from the Indian side of the LOC (Line of Control).

Significantly, President Clinton acted within two days of his talks with Nawaz Sharif on the Kargil conflict. Peace on the Sub-continent, therefore, is on the President's agenda. The joint statement issued by Nawaz Sharif and President Clinton in Washington on July 5, 1999 is a manifestation of the increasingly significant role that the US thinks itself destined to play in what it regards to be potential areas of conflict.

Pakistan's Kargil adventure has evoked a negative response from the Clinton Administration. Fearing a nuclear catastrophe it has clearly if not very vocally come down on India's side and exerted considerable pressure on Pakistan to withdraw from the conflict. In effect the crisis intensified the US tilt towards India, which has displayed restraint and maturity in its response towards Pakistan's aggressiveness.

To sum up, the conflagration in Kargil and Drass provided the perfect opening for Washington. The route from Kargil leads to Kashmir. The joint statement has crystallized the Kashmir dilemma. After the US succeeds in its efforts to persuade Pakistan to withdraw its forces, the US can no longer be denied a place in the process, though not as a mediator. According to Stephen Cohen "the US has a specific role between the two sides - faciliator"[21].

One may call it mediation, but facilitation is also a form of mediation, which prods policy planners in India to draw a long-term security and diplomatic strategy. Moreover, the implications of Kargil are being assessed by the presence of Private Armies enjoying the official military patronage in Pakistan is crucial in the context of security and stability of not only the sub continent but entire Asia.

Nuclear Policy of India

Peace movements took many years to develop in Western countries following nuclear weaponisation and even then these did not seek the elimination of the nuclear arsenals of the countries concerned in most cases. When sections of the British Labour Party leadership proposed that Britain should unilaterally abandon its nuclear arsenal, the British electorate taught the Labour Party a lesson they can never forget. India is the only country which in the wake of nuclearisation, continued - in the Rome Conference - to press for the setting up of an international criminal court of justice, making the use of nuclear weapons a crime against humanity, with those guilty of it to be tried by an international criminal court of justice.

We are living in a world in which the international community of 188 nations has decided to legitimize nuclear weapons by extending indefinitely and unconditionally the Non-Proliferation Treaty. It is popularly believed that Japan has great aversion to nuclear weapons, as it is the only country, which has ever been subjected to a nuclear attack. Therefore it puzzles Indians why Japan then voted to legitimize nuclear weapons and voted against them being considered a crime against humanity. Why does Japan need the protection of US nuclear deterrents even after the Cold War has ended and China is being engaged constructively by both the US and Japan? Similarly the non-aligned nations have declared themselves against nuclear weapons for well over three decades. Yet they agreed to legitimize the nuclear arsenals of five nuclear weapon powers through the indefinite and unconditional extensions of the Non-Proliferation Treaty. The five nuclear weapons powers accepted an obligation to negotiate in good faith, effective measures relating to cessation of the nuclear arms race at an early date, and for nuclear disarmament. Nothing was done in the first twenty five years before the NPT was extended indefinitely and unconditionally. In the two preparatory meetings held for the first quinquennial review conference to be held in 2000 A.D. no progress has been registered at all. There is a wide divergence between what nations preach and what they practice on the issue of nuclear weapons.

Nuclear threats to nations of the world can be averted only in one of two ways. Either the nuclear weapons should be prohibited and eliminated as is being done for two other categories of weapons of mass destructions - the biological and chemical, or nations should develop a balance of mutual deterrence which will reduce the risks of temptations to the five most war prone powers who are the acknowledged possessors of nuclear weapons today. India, having to register even the slightest advance on nuclear disarmament felt compelled to opt for the second alternative.

No doubt India has been highly critical of both the doctrine of nuclear deterrence as practised by the nuclear weapon powers as well as the balance of power strategy as expounded in the nineteenth and early twentieth centuries. The intrinsic merits and demerits of these strategies are not very relevant for pursuit of Indian foreign and security policies. What is of utmost relevance is that the world powers that count in global decision-making are pursing these strategies whether they are right or wrong. As long as India did not possess adequate military, economic and technological power to make an impact on the global system the international power game was bound to be played according to the rules prescribed by the major military and industrial powers of the world. India's choice was limited to being totally marginalized or joining the game and playing it as per the present rules. The rest of the non-aligned countries in spite of all their declaratory policies on disarmament and autonomy of nations were not able to stand up to the pressures of the industrialized world. Therefore, they endorsed the NPT and legitimized nuclear weapons. They adopted the CTBT with its entry into force clause which violated Vienna Convention on the law of the treaties and attempted to force the CTBT on India, after New Delhi had made it clear that it would not sign. Non-alignment was robbed of most of its content with these two treaties. The first coerced the non-aligned nations to endorse the legitimacy of nuclear weapons. The treaty exposed that they did not have the strength to stand up to defend the autonomy of decision-making of the developing nations. This is, today, the objective reality regarding most non-aligned nations. In these circumstances India had to opt or reinforce the balance of power in the global system and thereby provide an increased degree of autonomy of functioning to other members of international community. That is why the Indian dilemma on weapons was finally resolved with India exercising the nuclear option.

On May 11, 1998, two events took place:

(i) India carried out nuclear tests, and

(ii) India declared itself to be a state with nuclear weapons

The first demonstrated continuity in the policy of building the technological and material capabilities for an independent credible nuclear deterrence. This was in keeping with the 1964 commitment. India had successfully demonstrated its ability to explode a nuclear device in May 1974. To that extent, the five tests in 1998 only emphasized the continuity and growth of capability over the years. The tests were strongly criticized as expected, by the nuclear weapons states and their undeclared nuclear military allies. The point to remember is that while people may detest India's nuclear tests, the done cannot be undone.

India declaring itself to be a nuclear weapon state (SNW) has far reaching implications. This was an apparent departure from the decades' old policy. To most Indians it seems strange that the slow but sure march of their country towards nuclearization is seen with such surprise. It may sound strange now but India in the 40's and 50's did not exhibit' strategies to make itself secure, i.e. did not develop a strategy, which identifies the objectives that produce security, nor did it lay down those political and military determinants which could lead to or gain for it the security goals. In other words the concept of a Grand Strategy is a "political military means-ends chains, a state's theory about how it can best 'cause' security for itself". Under Nehrus "World Order Idealism" threat was not perceived from states but from the collective global problems like poverty, imperialistic domination, ideology and religious fundamentalism, hegemony of nuclear powers and so on. He therefore directed his efforts in bringing about a fundamental transformation of the existing state system into a humanitarian world order through disarmament. The 1962 Sino-India War and the humiliations that India had to suffer shattered Nehru and his belief[22].

And he had hoped that:

> India would develop atomic power for peaceful uses but warned that as long the world was constituted as it was, every country would have to develop and use the latest scientific devices for its protection".[23]

It may be useful to briefly review India's progress to becoming an SNW in order to ascertain its motivations. The Sino Indian war of 1962 had left a deep impact on Indian society and leadership and the scars have not healed yet. One day after the tests the Prime Minister wrote to the US president:

> "I have been deeply concerned at the deteriorating security environment, especially the nuclear environment, faced by India for some years past. We have an overt nuclear weapons state on our borders a state which committed armed aggression against India in 1962. Although our relations with that country have improved in the last decade or so atmosphere of distrust persists mainly due to the unresolved border problem. To add to the distrust that country has materially helped another neighbour of ours to become a covert nuclear weapon state. At the hands of this bitter neighbour we have suffered three aggressions in the past fifty years[24].

Bhartiya Janata Party started demanding nuclear weapons for India from that time. Indian National Congress also considered the question of acquiring nuclear weapons after the Chinese test in 1964, but persuaded itself to deter the decision. Prime Minister Lal Bahadur Shastri provided a definite thrust to nuclearisation at a future date and launched a programme to reduce the time needed to build nuclear arms to six months[25].

At the same time, dialogue was initiated with the UK and in 1966-67 with the USSR and the United States. These parleys did not lead to any definitive results and the US made it clear that no nuclear guarantees to India (essentially against China which was a Communist country not even recognized by the United States) could be provided. India had to stand alone and independent in matters of national security[26].

The armed conflict with Pakistan in 1967 reinforced this view. India had been a co-sponsor of the UN General Assembly resolution of November 19, 1967, which sought a nuclear Non-Proliferation Treaty (NPT) that would carry a balance of obligations between the nuclear weapon states and those expected not to acquire any weapon. But the actual treaty evolved with a heavy bias in favour of non-proliferation and a mild clause for nuclear disarmament, which has not been fulfilled even three decades later.

The prospects of a war in 1971 generated a more immediate concern in India which did not have the force levels to be deployed on three fronts concurrently that is West Pakistan, East Pakistan (where the Pakistan Army had sought to launch an offensive into India in April May 1971) and the northern borders with China. This led to the Indo-Soviet Treaty of August 1971, a treaty that India had resisted for a number of years. Even more important, the treaty also incorporated a clause for mutual consultations if the security of either was threatened. In the event, China unlike its policy in 1965, remained non-interventionist. But the United States despatched, a nuclear-armed armada led by the US 'Enterprise' to coerce New Delhi[27].

The latter saw not only the tilt in favour of Pakistan but also the potential nuclear coercion, although actual use was not seen as a credible scenario[28]. This experience reinforced the will to have an independent deterrent.

It is now well known that the then Prime Minister Indira Gandhi gave instructions in 1972 for the nuclear test (a peaceful nuclear explosion) carried out in 1974. Upto this stage, Pakistan while taken seriously in terms of its conventional capability was not seen as a factor in any nuclear security calculus in the region. In fact, even Jammu and Kashmir was not a factor defining the security relationship between India and Pakistan for two decades after 1966. It was the phenomenon of Soviet intervention in Afghanistan in 1979 and even more important, Pakistan's willingness to accept the role of a "front line state" in 1981, that brought about a change in the Indian security paradigms.

In more recent times, the demands for exercising the nuclear option and overt nuclearisation had been growing, especially during the 1990s. The position adopted with regard to the Comprehensive Test Ban Treaty (CTBT) in 1996, articulated national security as a major reason for not signing it. There were a number of options in the manner and method of exercising the nuclear option kept open clearly as a deliberate policy since at least 1964[29].

These related essentially to the choices that would provide the optimum cost-benefit ratios but did not deviate from the central issue and the growing consensus that exercising the nuclear option had now become almost inevitable. This had less to do with any immediate military threat and a more to do with assessment of how to maintain the minimum level of strategic capabilities, which remain credible and flexible to meet the strategic uncertainties of the future. It is in this context that the tests became useful in that they indicated the resolve and the technological prowess to provide necessary credibility for deterrence.

An examination of India's nuclear policy as it has evolved over the decades and especially during the past one year requires that we first address the question: Why does India need nuclear weapons?

India does not require nuclear weapons for prestige or status, although nuclear weapons have been seen as the currency of power since Hiroshima. Our prestige will be governed by our ability to solve our problems successfully. The issue of national security in relation to nuclear weapon threat is one of those myriad problems. For a country pursuing an independent foreign and security policy, potential challenges posed by existing technical and specific nuclear weapons threat can be adequately addressed only-:

(i) Through global abolition of nuclear weapons, or

(ii) By reliance on nuclear deterrence to ward off such challenges. The latter could be autonomous or provided by military alliances (as is the case for a large number of countries).

The Indian leadership had decided long before independence that the country would pursue an independent and non-aligned foreign and defence policy[30].

Contrary to conventional wisdom, the Cold War was neither the sole nor the most critical reference point of non-alignment which emanated and grew in a wider complex of national and international factors in the post World War II period. The central factors that pushed India toward overt nuclear weapons deterrence can be seen under seven heads: -

1. The China Factor
2. Enhanced Nuclear Proliferation
3. Eroding prospects of Disarmament
4. Dominant strategic Doctrines
5. Post Cold War International Order
6. Threat to Nuclear Option
7. The CTBT Deadline

Not only has nuclear disarmament been seen in India as the only comprehensive and durable non-proliferation instrument, but nuclear disarmament has been a key strategic and security goal for it. India's preferred options, not unsurprisingly, was to keep the nuclear option open as long as feasible, not weaponise and work for disarmament which would eliminate the roots of the nuclear security dilemma. This was mostly ignored or perhaps not understood in the Western world as a strategy of restraint. It was seen more as a policy of weakness and a challenge to the non-proliferation order, which was being expanded and deepened. For India an "Open option" represented an optimum policy, which minimized costs and maximized capabilities[31].

But after 1990, stimulated by the Iraqi quest for nuclear weapons[32], the weapon states partly to protect their own weapon status, set renewed vigour on the path of non-proliferation, seeking to roll back India's nuclear programme. The basic logic of the renewed focus of non-proliferation may have been global in nature, with selective targeting of the "rogue states, but India also specifically targetted although the international community was polite enough not to refer to India as a " rogue state"!

What are the main tenets of Indian strategic policy based on the doctrine of nuclear deterrence? Some of the important tenets of Minimal Nuclear Deterrence-it is referred as MIND-can be underscored here.

First and the foremost, India is firmly committed to the principle of "no first use" of nuclear weapons. India has already offered to sign such a treaty with Pakistan; who has off-hand rejected the proposal by declaring it as" self serving". It sees nuclear weapons as a credible deterrence in view of India's conventional superiority".

Secondly India will not resort to the use of nuclear weapons against states, which are not aligned[33], or with the NWS. This principle needs to be seen in the context of Indian nuclear weapons being for self-defence. This is to be seen in the context of the US threat to use nuclear weapons even against NNWS. Within South Asia, no state other than Pakistan has ever expressed any apprehension from India's nuclear weapons.

Thirdly, in the event of failure of nuclear deterrence, and if India is attacked with nuclear weapons India will use nuclear weapons in a second strike "to retaliate and to inflict damage unacceptable to the aggressor". The credibility of such deterrence will depend upon sufficiency of nuclear weapons.

Fourthly, India needs to concentrate to make is nuclear weapons invulnerable to first strike with nuclear weapon either by Pakistan or China or jointly by them. The Nuclear Doctrine speaks of a triad of aircraft, land based, mobile missiles Agni II (2,500 km) and Agni III (3,500 km) - is essential but India also needs to focus on its perfection to the extent that at least half of the missiles fired will hit the target within a radius of a mile or two. To make nuclear weapons invulnerable to first strike, India will also have to develop nuclear submarines and deploy anti ballistic missiles.

Fifthly, MIND also assures civilian control of nuclear weapons by a democratically elected leadership through a system of command and control. The ultimate decision to use the nuclear weapons will rest with the Prime-Minister. But in a worst case scenario, there is the need to clearly lay down the alternate democratic chain of command in the event of conflict escalating into a war.

Similarly, if New Delhi is made dysfunctional by enemy bombing from where will the command and control operate? How do you carry nuclear weapons to enemy targets? Do you use aircraft or missiles or submarines or use the tactical nuclear weapons? In other words, it is also necessary to resolve the question of any possible inter service rivalry on the possession of nuclear weapons, creation of a Chief of Defence Staff assumes additional urgency. The doctrine also promises an integrated plan of "command, control, communications, intelligence and information (C412)".

Sixthly, India will also develop or acquire the necessary protective safety systems for nuclear weapons. This will prevent triggering of any accidental war, or unauthorised use of nuclear weapons. It also stresses adequate provisions for avoiding theft or sabotage of nuclear weapons systems.

Seventhly, "to raise the threshold of outbreak of both conventional and military conflicts as well as that of threat or use of nuclear weapons", India will maintain "highly effective conventional military capabilities...". It means that in the near future India will not be able to reduce the size of its armed forces because of acquisition of nuclear weapon though eventually that is a possibility as the threat to India's security will continue to arise from Pakistan mainly through low intensity conflict (LIC) in fulfillment of the religiously emotive issue of completion of the incomplete partition process in Kashmir as was the case in the Kargil conflict.

It is possible for India to reduce armed forces on the Sino-Indian borders, without much reservation though a bilateral agreement. But it is necessary for India to move in the direction of equipping the armed forces for technological warfare.

Next, the doctrine also reassures the Indian nuclear establishment that it will continue to "step up efforts in research and development to keep up with technological advances in this field". While India has no plans to go in for the production of neutron bombs[34], it cannot accept any limitations on developing its R & D capability.

Finally, India will continue to emphasize - from a position of strength, global nuclear disarmament. The doctrine believes that "global verifiable and non-discriminatory nuclear disarmament is a national security objective". Even after acquisition of nuclear weapons, Indian strategy is not based on the use of nuclear weapons. On the other hand India now sees that it can speak on nuclear disarmament there is a need to move gradually towards it. Hence a successful conclusion of a no first use treaty as a first step will greatly reduce the threat of nuclear war.

Though, with the disintegration of the Soviet Union, there was an end of the cold war within the global triangle and consequent breakdown of the South Asian regional pentagon there was no end to the cold war in South Asia. India-Pakistan conflicts continued and so did the Sino-Pakistan cooperation in the national security arena. The report of the Indian Parliamentary Committee on Defence of 1995 states:

China has also continued to be the main source of major weapons, including missiles and allied technology to Pakistan, a very hostile neighbour causing disquiet to India. Despite warming relations with China, China is and is likely to remain the primary security challenge to India in the medium and long terms. Its enhancement of missile capabilities and its immense help to Pakistan in the missile programme are serious security concerns to India[35].

If any country could have stopped the slow drift towards an overt nuclearisation of the Subcontinent and possible war, it was the US. But the US had its own irons in the fire. In the immediate aftermath of the cold war many Indians had hoped that the two countries would rediscover the warmth that had marked the Roosevelt and Kennedy years (when the US had consistently championed India's freedom). But that was not to be. Deprived of its central focus, American foreign policy splintered into a series of uncoordinated initiatives pushed by the territorial and functional bureaus of the State Department, which as often as not saw themselves in competition with each other.

President Bill Clinton himself set the tone for the US criticism of the Indian tests when he characterized them as a "terrible mistake"[36]. He also said that, "with democratic traditions the nuclear path is not the way of greatness"[37]?

Madeleine Albright the American Minister of State was speaking like a school headmistress, when she said in a TV interview on June 20, "We want to make them understand that they cannot blast their way into nuclear status"[38]. The State Department spokesman, James Rubin, accused the Indian Government of being deceitful in its dealing with the US on the nuclear issues. He accused India of lying and conducting a "campaign of duplicity" during twenty high level meetings between the two countries.

It is independently confirmed by more than one governmental source in the US 'President Clintons' policy of "cap, reduce, and eliminate" nuclear capabilities in South Asia implied that eventually the two countries would have to give up their nuclear capabilities and that the present policy was merely a way station on the road to complete regional disarmament (without any commitment to applying such a policy to existing nuclear weapon states)[39]. But since Pakistan had pursued a policy based on the premise that it will do whatever India does the US policy essentially targeted only India.

In 1993 the Clinton Administration had imposed partial economic sanctions against China for supplying M-11 missile parts to Pakistan. But these were withdrawn under duress in October 1994. In return, China promised to adhere to the US sponsored Missile Transfer Control Regime (MTCR) only to renege on it in May 1999 as it had certain commitments[40].

The US also, during the post cold war period played different patterns of roles in its relations with India. Without going into details during nearly seven years of the Clinton Administration, US India relations went through periods of ups and downs and also touched a plateau in between, particularly on nuclear related issue. The Administration started by applying public pressures on India first to cap, then roll back and finally eliminate its nuclear programme (January 1993 to May 1994).

An insecurity dilemma was created in the minds of Indian policy makers by drawing attention to Pakistan's linking its own nuclear programme to its unresolved Kashmir dispute. Pressure was also brought to bear on India to sign the nuclear Non-Proliferation Treaty (NPT). Similar pressure was applied over the issue of human right in the Punjab and Kashmir.

After the then Prime Minister Narasimha Rao's visit to Washington, public pressure on India on vital security issues was suspended in return for Rao's promise not to create problems for the US at the NPT review conference in New York, and go along with the US on the issues like the Comprehensive Test Ban Treaty (CTBT) and the proposed Fissile, Materials Cut off Treaty (FMCT)[41].

However, the US also, on its part promised not to sell weapons to Pakistan. But by mid-October 1995, President Clinton personally asked the Senate to make a one-time exception to the Pressler Amendment, which bans sale of weapons to Pakistan to provide $368 million worth of weapons to that country. This was done under the flank Amendment to the Pressler Amendment. Since then the relations between the two had reached a plateau, and Prime Minister Rao as the elections of 1996 began to draw near, categorically stated that India will retain its nuclear option.

The US was also pushing for the CTBT by 1996, clearly as a non-proliferation measure while India had joined in the promotion of the treaty as a nuclear disarmament measure. The US approach was best expressed by John D. Holum, then director of the US Arms Control and Disarmament Agency, on November 2, 1995, in an address at Georgetown University. He made it implicity clear that the aim of the CTBT is to prevent India from acquiring nuclear weapons when he said that the CTBT will stem proliferation by preventing others countries from moving beyond the most rudimentary devices.... "The United States has conducted well over 1,000 nuclear tests - hundred more than any country. The value to US of any tiny increment in knowledge from more tests is heavily out weighed by the value of preventing tests by others, including rogue states who could derive quantum leaps of capability from even a few tests"[42]. In the light of the above national security threat to India, the country once again needed to be self - reliant for maintaining its national security. These developments eventually made India decide in favour of conducting nuclear tests in May 1998.

Had India and Pakistan been two ordinary countries the rapid development of a new US Pakistan axis would not have effected Washington's ties with New Delhi. But the Kashmir dispute and Kargil war made that impossible. The Clinton Administration was forced to choose and decided in favour of Pakistan once more. The reason was that while it sought to build its post cold war ties with India on the base of shared ideals, such as a commitment to democracy and the creation of an open market friendly economy, it was building its relations with Pakistan on realpolitik. Slowly but surely, realpolitik won out.

Nuclear Policy of Pakistan

Pakistan's nuclear policy reveals an evolving pattern of rapid, dedicated nuclear development encompassing development of both plutonium and enriched uranium bomb routes to proliferation, but these developments are not phased, deterministic or inevitable. It is not enough to say what nuclear policy is about and what nexus it has with foreign policy. It may be relevant to ask more questions analysing nuclear policy, for instance, is there such a thing as a single coherent orchestrated and national nuclear policy? Are we really dealing with a series of disjointed, finite and often mutually conflicting, policies emerging from different governmental levels and divisions that are responding piecemeal to their own narrow focused problems?

Theoretically, it may be stated that a policy can exist in a coherent means-ends form, its objectives can be defined and means for their pursuit specified.

Pakistani nuclear activities and its nuclear posture reveal a sensitivity, indeed a vulnerability to the attitudes and style of its political leadership, to constraints derived from Pakistan's conditions and finally to the impact of the regional strategic environment and domestic public opinion. Thus evolving domestic, regional, international settings have an impact on the lines of development of Pakistan's nuclear capabilities and its incentives and disincentives.

Many analysts have argued that Pakistan's nuclear programme has emanated 'solely as a reaction to India's nuclear activities. Pervaiz Iqbal Cheema a Pakistani analyst has argued that "Pakistan's nuclear choices are directly or indirectly linked with the developments in the region, more specially India's, nuclear policy"[43].

In addition to this context Gen. Pervez Musharraf, while speaking at the UAE Armed Forces Day reception, said, "The range of our Ghauri-II missile is 2,200 km at present, and we have not decided as to what range we are going to achieve ultimately. Our security concern is oriented against our eastern neighbour and nobody else.". He added "However if some threat is posed to us from any other quarter then our security concerns would get involved. Basically at the moment our security concern is oriented against our immediate neighbour"[44]

Anti India orientation has not always been of primary importance in Pakistani nuclear activities. It was Bhutto who gave an anti-India stance to Pakistan's nuclear weapon programme in his diplomacy to build Islamic links and to broaden the base of Pakistan's security.

Zulfikar Ali Bhutto was, in fact, the chief architect of Pakistan's nuclear policy and its nuclear programme. Single handed and with great determination, he built up the nuclear programme from almost scratch to a viable deterrent capability.

Significantly, the Pakistani nuclear doctrine - the use of a nuclear ultimatum as an instrument of unilaterally containing India retribution has been pursued by all governments in Islamabad since the early 1990s. During a visit to Kashmir, Nawaz Sharif, the former Prime Minister of Pakistan, declared that Pakistan was a nuclear power, "I confirm Pakistan, possesses the atomic bomb", he stated. He then warned India that an attack on Pakistan could trigger a nuclear war.

Further more, Sharif anticipated an escalation of the crisis over Kashmir because of India's refusal to surrender Kashmir to Pakistan. Nawaz was perhaps the most authoritative Pakistani to confirm the nuclear power status of Pakistan but he was not the first. The present world-view of Islamabad is a direct continuation of the vision of Mr. Zulfikar Ali Bhutto.

The political vision of Bhutto was crystallized as a historical legacy of the 1971 dismemberment of Pakistan. The new Pakistan must base its policy on Islamic character and look west words to the hub of Islam - for identity and belonging. He considered Central Asia an extension of the non-Arab Muslim World that Pakistan would bring with it to the hub in the order to expand its non-Arab component. The active support for the armed liberation struggle in Kashmir was defined by Bhutto as a major way of proving and demonstrating Pakistan's commitment to Islamic solidarity and values. Extremely close strategic relations with the PRC, including, Beijing's strategic guarantees and assistance in the development of Pakistan's nuclear weapons, were considered the foundations of

Islamabad's ability to deter an inevitable clash with the US and a possible war with India.

Pakistan was looking into the acquisition of nuclear weapons since the early - 1960s. After Pakistan's defeat in the 1965 Indo-Pakistani war, Zulfikar Ali Bhutto vowed to retain a strategic balance with India, including the development of nuclear weapons, at any cost. "If India builds the bomb, we will eat grass or leaves, even go hungry, but we will get one of our own. We have no alternative", Bhutto declared in 1965. But it had to accept the humiliating defeat of 1971, when Indian forces occupied Eastern Pakistan to the acquisition of nuclear weapons. Mr. Bhutto delivered a passionate speech about the shame of defeat and how imperative it was for Pakistan to have nuclear weapons. Bhutto pointed to a higher objective when he explained that "this is a very serious political decision, which Pakistan must take and perhaps all Third World countries must take one day because it is coming", Pakistan thus committed itself to a national crash programme to have an Islamic Bomb. The Pakistani nuclear bomb programme really took off in 1974 when Dr. Abdul Qadeer Khan returned to Pakistan from Europe and convinced Bhutto that he could build a bomb. Bhutto secured PRC's agreement to support the Pakistani military nuclear programme. Using Chinese weapons technology, Dr. Khan laid the solid foundations of the Pakistani nuclear weapons.

Gen. Zia Ul-Haq rose to power in the 1977 military coup. It was during his 11-year tenure that Pakistan became a nuclear power and defined a coherent nuclear strategy. The military that seized power in 1977 opposed to the nuclear weapons programme, fearing the impact of the drainage of resources. However, there was a wide spread recognition that nuclear weapons were Pakistan's only viable deterrence against an Indian conventional onslaught. Some strategists even urged the recapture of Kashmir under a nuclear umbrella. Zia became committed to the nuclear option as a last resort instrument to save Pakistan" with the whole world against him", an argument made by Agha Shahi, the then Foreign Minister. In July 1978,

Zia outlined his perception: "China, India, the USSR and Isreal in the Middle East posses the atomic arm. No Muslim country has any. If Pakistan had such a weapon, it would reinforce the power of the Muslim World."

Pakistan had nuclear weapons potential in 1988. However, at the same time Zia-ul-Haq's pan-Islamic World-view was expressed in the willingness to facilitate and expedite other Islamic countries, primarily Iran's nuclear weapons programme, but not at the expense of or as part of Pakistan's own strategic weapons programmes. It was through its close cooperation with Iran, that Pakistan also assisted other radical states including Libya, and North Korea.

Soon afterwards, Pakistan began a game of brinkmanship through the escalation of border clashed in the Siachen Glacier area in the Kashmir-Pakistani active support for the Islamist insurgency in Kashmir increased markedly. The near war appearance of a major Indian military exercise not far from the Pakistani High Command, reminding them of the possibility of a massive Indian reaction to the Pakistan provocations. At the same time, the border clashes and the intrust on of terrorists into Indian Kashmir continued to escalate. Meanwhile, the overall Pakistani strategic confidence was already expressed in brinkmanship statements coming out of Islamabad since the fall of 1993. For example, Qazi Hussain Ahmad, the Jamaat I-Islami Chief Senator, urged the Benazir Bhutto government to declare Jihad on India to save Kashmiri Muslims from total annihilation". There is no other way to resolve the crisis, he declared "Let us wage Jihad for Kashmir. A nuclear armed Pakistan would deter India from a wider conflict", he stressed. Mrs. Bhutto was fully aware of her country's nuclear potential because she served as the chairperson of the National Nuclear Command Authority (NNCA). The NNCA determines the state of readiness of the Pakistani nuclear weapons and with Mrs. Bhutto's hand on the button authorizes their launch through the Army's Joint Operations Centre. Gen Beg disclosed in April 1994 that Pakistan already has "the F-16s, Mirages and M-11 (ballistic missiles) which we are now getting from China that can carry nuclear weapons". Moreover, Pakistani's own missile programme is developing a delivery system with a very effective accurate guiding system provided on the missiles. Called the Anza-11, this ballistic missile is a Pakistani derivative of the Chinese M-11, One Pakistani official confirmed that the development Anza-11 is being accelerated with Chinese assistance". Visiting Pakistani's nuclear enrichment facility in Multan, Mrs. Bhutto warned of accelerating "missile race" in the region and assured that the PRC would provide Pakistan with all the necessary technology and know-how to cope with the new strategic challenge. N.D. Khan, the Parliamentary Secretary for Foreign Affairs and other Pakistani senior officials stressed repeatedly that Pakistan will not curtail its nuclear programme irrespective of mounting US pressure. Instead the High Command announced that Pakistan has embarked on a major build up of sophisticated weapons including missiles, in order to deal with any emergency in the context of the India's aggressive designs". Mrs. Bhutto was briefed on this emergency massive programme and "agreed in principle to meet the requirements of the Pakistani Army on urgent basis". Indeed Pakistani officials later confirmed that Islamabad has resolved, "to manufacture (ballistic) missiles and strengthen its defense".

The former President of Pakistan, Farooq Ahmed Khan Leghari visited the Pakistani Air Force (PAF) base in Sargodha, home of the P-16s to inspect the major exercise called Saffron Bandit - 94. In a speech to the PAP officers he tied together the current military build up and the crisis in Kashmir. Leghari assured his audience that "the government is fully aware of the defense needs of the country and will equip its Armed Forces with sophisticated weapons for the defense of the motherland". Leghari reiterated Islamabad's full support to the Kashmiri people despite Indian threats and stressed his confidence that Pakistan can meet any threat" resulting from this strategy.

Pakistan has also intensified its work on a new generation of plutonium-based weapons using know-how provided by the PRC, Iran and North Korea. Such close cooperation in nuclear development is not surprising. The PRC was the primary source of technology and know-how for Pakistan's first generation of uranium-based nuclear weapons in the 1980s. Since the late 1980s Iran has also closely cooperated with the Pakistani nuclear effort. From the early 1990 Iran has shared with Pakistan, Iraqi data Tehran had acquired directly and from Hussayn-al-Sharistani who resurfaced in Iran in 1991, after the Gulf War and has since visited Pakistan, Iran and DPRK and run several strategic weapons joint programmes, including the development of plutonium-based nuclear warheads using clandestinely delivered Chinese technology and sub-system. Plutonium-based warheads of the type used by the PRC and its allies are about 50 kt. strong, and can fit on M-11 type ballistic missiles.

Meanwhile, the nuclear strategy of Bhutto's Pakistan was being refined and better defined. Islamabad was now convinced that only nuclear deterrence can prevent an Indian offensive from defeating the Pakistani Army. Mrs. Bhutto stressed the centrality of the nuclear component to Pakistan's overall war-fighting capabilities: "Only in the presence of a nuclear deterrent can the Pakistani Army feel strong and stable. Confronting India with conventional weapons especially when these weapons have been provided by a superpower like the US would not only be difficult but would be tantamount to inviting danger as well". These statements are most apprehensive about a scenario where New Delhi will interpret Pakistani mobilization intended as a "signal" in the brinkmanship policy for Pakistani domestic purposes-as actual preparations for war. India may than launch a conventional preemption against Pakistani forces concentrated and forward deployed during the brinkmanship and near-war phases. Pakistani Islamist senior officials are convinced that the Pakistani Armed Forces will collapse if such an Indian offensive is allowed to develop fully. Given the mounting internal pressures inside Pakistan, the first signs of defeat may very well cause a popular eruption and the self-destruction of Pakistan. Therefore, it is imperative for Pakistan to acquire long-range nuclear strike capabilities in order to contain and deter any potential Indian reaction to the mounting provocations, escalating terrorism and overall policy of brinkmanship. Taken together, Islamabad is pushing South Asia into a most unstable situation fraught with great dangers. The Islamist circles of power in Islamabad continue to increase their sponsorship of terrorism and subversion in India while hyping the fears of an Indian offensive for domestic political needs inside Islamabad. Anticipating and sponsoring a major escalation of Islamist terrorism and subversion in Kashmir in the spring, once the weather improves, Islamabad is increasingly apprehensive about the potential Indian reaction to the escalatory spiral.

Islamabad is urging an all Muslim response to the growing regional threat from India. The Indian oppression of Muslims in Kashmir, Islamabad stresses, is only the beginning of a Hindu onslaught on Islam. "Since India is against the world of Islams, explained a Pakistani official, "it is the duty of the Muslim Ummah (nation / community) to forge unity among its ranks, to pool its resources and to turn itself into an impregnable fortress to counter the threat of Hindu imperialism. The mere adoption of this strategy clearly reflects the growing power and influence of the Islamist circles in Islamabad. These circles are committed to enhancing Pakistani's active participation in the regional surges of both the Beijing led Trans Asian Axis and particularly the Teheran led Islamic bloc.

Pakistan has had a crucial role in the PRC's strategic contingency plans. The PLA consider India as "the greatest potential threat" for PRC itself because the implementation of the PRC's Trans-Asian Axis strategy endangers India's vital interests and thus might very well lead to a military clash. The PLA stresses that they "see India as a potential adversary mainly because India's strategic focus remains on the Indian Ocean and Southeast Asia". Therefore, for the PRC to further its strategic surge westward both in the heart of Asia and on the spaces of the Indian Ocean", it is imperative for the PRC to divert India's strategic attention away from Chinese strategic surge. The role of Pakistan in the Chinese grand design is instigating this strategic diversion. Pakistan should create a major defense challenge to India from the west using a myriad of instruments ranging from subversion to a major military build up. According to the PRC's strategic designs the aggregate effect of this Pakistani strategy should be a growing tension along the Indo-Pakistan border that would compel New Delhi to concentrate on meeting the Pakistani challenge as a national priority and thus neglect blocking the PRC's westward surge until it is too late to reverse the new geo-strategic realities in Asia.

On April 25, 1998 Pakistan announced that it had tested two missiles, one having a range of 80 km and the other 300 km. These missiles, the Hatf-I and Hatf - II, are claimed to have a capacity to lift a 500 kg load. The former is believed to have been, deployed in December 1989, while the latter was displayed during the Pakistan pay parade the same year. Some however believe that the Hatf is not a missile but a rocket[45].

Pakistan set up a Missile Development Board in 1992 with active assistance from SUPARCO. A successful test of the third missile Hatf -III which is a two stage solid propellant, having a range of 600 km and play load capacity ropelleant, of 500 kg, was conducted by SUPARCO, the civilian space research organisation in July, 1997[46].

In April 1998, Pakistan test fired a medium range ballistic missile, the Ghauri. The missile has a range of 1,500 km and a payload capacity of 700 kg. The fact that the missile, was "proven" already. It is believed to be derived from the Dong-Teng-35 of China or North Korea's Nodong-2. Shaheen, a 700 km range missile was successfully test fired in 1999. There are reports of development of a still longer range Ghaznavi (2,000 km) missiles by Pakistan. The MTCR has been totally ineffective in curbing Pakistan's missiles programme, indigenous content not with standing. In fact, as shall be seen subsequently, the same is, the case where missile acquisition is concerned the MTCR has been totally ineffective.

Recent nuclear tests by India and Pakistan have stunned the world in general, and the US in particular. The reactive and negative response from the West led by the US, the sole super power, is neither unexpected nor surprising. In order to counter the challenge of nuclerarisation in South Asia, the US has adopted a 3-pronged strategy, which includes:

1. Internationalisation of Kashmir dispute,
2. Involvement of the China in the affairs of South Asia especially in nuclear affairs, and
3. Economic sanctions.

Kashmir dispute: The Sub-continent's 'blast for blast' diplomacy has underscored the need to refocus attention on the tensions in the fifty year old Kashmir dispute. Spelling out the American policy on Kashmir, Deputy Secretary of State, Strobe Talbott, in an interview to the Far Eastern Economic Review said, "the US would urge the UN to play a constructive role in resolving the issue which has been on its agenda since the birth of India, the birth of Pakistan and the birth of UN. After the detonation of nuclear devices by India and Pakistan, the US has been chiefly instrumental in bringing back Kashmir on the international agenda". The reference to the Kashmir issue in statements of the P-5 G-8 and the UN Security Council bear testimony to this. The permanent members of the UN Security Council led by the US argued that the risk of conflict over Kashmir has multiplied manifold, by the acquisition of nuclear weapons and therefore they have a duty to intervene.

Chinese involvement: In the US scheme, China is emerging as a central player in managing the turbulence in South Asia. President Clinton expressed that Beijing must be associated with the ultimate solution of the problems between India and Pakistan including Kashmir. He added, I will work with President Jiang to advance our Asian Security agenda, keeping the pressure on India and Pakistan to curb their nuclear arms race power with increasingly sophisticated industrial and technological capabilities, China can choose either to be the part of the problem, or part of the solution. US is trying its best to whitewash the role of China's proliferation of missiles and nuclear weapons components to Pakistan has played in pushing the sub-continent towards nuclearisation.

Economic Sanctions: The imposition of sanctions by the US on India and Pakistan is automatic under the Glenn amendment. The Clinton Administration's announcement of comprehensive sanctions were meant to penalise India and Pakistan for nuclear testing. The suspicion that the US may be contemplating to enforce tough and comprehensive economic sanctions against India in retaliation for its nuclear tests and going soft with Pakistan was laid to rest by Karl Indurfurth, Assistant Secretary of State for South Asian Affairs when he declared "There is no provision under the Glenn amendment for who tested first, who tested second or who was provoked". The mandatory US sanctions are bound to hurt Pakistan more seriously than India. But Pakistan has some leverage. It can step US narcotics exports to the US and Western Europe to ameliorate its financial conditions under the sanctions. After imposing the sanctions the US Secretary of State Albright warned other countries not to take advantage of the fact that Washington had imposed sanctions, on India and Pakistan because of nuclear tests. She said "while the US and other nuclear powers are already to assist them in settling differences and reducing tensions, Washington will maintain sanctions until this situation is resolved".

South Asian strategic reality is truly alarming. The tests have resulted in the nuclearisation of the region which has degraded security in numerous. The tests are now behind us so it serves no useful purpose whether they should have been done or not done. Washington should realise that internationalisation of the Kashmir dispute, involvement of China in South Asian affairs and the imposition of sanctions are not going to help in creating more tranquil circumstances in the Sub-continent. The US Administration will eventually have to reconcile itself to the nuclear ground realities in South Asia. This reality is irreversible through any measures but for the global disarmament.

Track Two Diplomacy

Since President Zia-ur-Rahman of Bangladesh circulated a letter proposing the establishment of the South Asian

Association for Regional Cooperation (SAARC) in 1980, the process of regional cooperation and conflict resolution has attracted the interest of the non-government community in South Asia. Many initiatives involving academics former government officials, grassroot workers, technical experts, the media, trade and industry have been launched to promote people to people confidence building measures. The rising awareness of the implications of the arms race, particularly in the nuclear sector, has recently led to a change in the emphasis from cooperation to conflict resolution.

The first step to achieve the objective of regional cooperation is to create an atmosphere of confidence, which would facilitate the ground for cooperation. The CSBMs are appropriate because they give operational and mechanical substance to the concept of security and to enhance the peace by generating confidence among people of hostile nations. The process of cooperation can be expedited if people of hostile nations get realistic approach of each others intentions and capabilities. Confidence can be enhanced by assurance about the goals, openness, transparency and predictability. The CBNM's are based on the idea of promoting the feeling of trust and confidence between hostile states or groups. The CSBMs can work only if the concerned parties have faith in the intentions of its adversary.

The goal of confidence and security building measures is to reduce or eliminate the cause of mistrust, fear, tensions and hostilities. But the most important aspect of CSBMs is to create a climate in which even the most complicated issues are subjected to analysis and discussion aimed at resolving them. Military CSBM's, such as the Indo-Pakistan agreements, not to strike each other's nuclear installations, to prevent air space violations, to permit over-flights and landings of military exercises and troop movements along mutual borders have substantially enhanced each country's notice of confidence in security affairs. Similar CSBM's in the political areana could lead to greater rationality and stability in relations between the two countries.

CSBM's fall into four general categories: mutual security pledges, transparency measures, managing dangerous and potentially dangerous military activities and crisis management measures. Transparency measures include the monitoring of military activities the stationing of observers at military bases, and the exchange of military data and information about a country's military doctrines. The range of crisis management devices and techniques include hotline between central military commands and direct contacts between local military authorities. CSBMs may also involve the prohibition or limitations of certain activities that are deemed to be provocative or dangerous. These can include restrictions on overflights of territory, the creation, demilitarized zones and the prior of notification of military exercises.

The CSBMs initiated on regional basis can lead to prevention of war and attainment of meaningful security. On 25th April 1990; Academics for peace in South Asia passed a resolution in New Delhi that stated that the "unity of the people of South Asia makes conciliation rather than confrontation the natural inclination of the people in the region regardless of the natural boundaries". The resolution further stated that the problem of South Asia cannot be solved by war and political institutions are capable of resolving conflicts. In spite of immense possibility of progress in the direction of regional cooperation, South Asia is still haunted by prejudices and suspicions which remain pervasive. The hardliners in various political parties, religious groups, segments of academicians journalists and establishments of both civilians and military, have proved counter productive to CSBM in South Asia.

Crisis management is an activity that political leaders, diplomats and soldiers have been engaged in since the emergence of organized state conflict. In the twentieth century, however, two factors have made crisis management both necessary and vital. The first is advent of the nuclear age and the devastating social annihilation that could result from the use of nuclear weapons. The second factor is the increasing recognition that normal organisational and operational processes come under severe stress during international crises. Crises are extraordinary situations between peace and war; where conflict between the national interest of two or more countries calls for action in a compressed time frame and involves the use or threat of force. Such crisis require coordination between military and political leaders in each country and often involve other nations as well.

In recent years a number of intriguing confidence and security enhancing measures have been proposed for India and Pakistan a regional cut off fissile material production, a regional nuclear test ban, the placement of new and existing nuclear facilities under safeguards extension of the nuclear no attack pledge to cover population centres, strengthened international security assurances regional risk reduction centres, expanded and upgraded hotlines between military and political officials and regular exchange of military personals[47]. The significant CSBM emplaced and how they could be further extended can now be noticed:

1. The agreement on non-attack of nuclear facilities was signed in December 1988 but ratified in January 1992 after the disintegrated facilities were exchanged by the two countries. Its scope could be further enlarged to include population and high value economic targets in the non-attack list;
2. The hot line established between the two DGMOS, apart from procedures for its operation could be extended to the Navies / Air Forces alongwith ensuring that multiple redundancy links are available to enable fail safe communications at all time,
3. The agreement on advance notice of military exercises, manoeuvres and troop movements ratified in 1992 (August) could be broadened in several directions. It could include information regarding deployment of offensive weapon system like armour within specified border zones to reduce opportunities for preemptive attacks. The association of military observers with such exercises is another such confidence building measure. This gains strength because

several recent military crisis in Indo-Pak relations have revolved around large scale military exercise e.g. Brasstacks (1986-87) Zarb-e-Momia (1989) and Indian troop movements in Kashmir (1990). A further agreement on the means to verify numbers would add immeasurably to confidence building between the two countries.

4. The agreement to prevent air space violations and permit overflights / landings by military aircrafts, signed in April 1991, could be extended into an "open skies" arrangement. It could undertake aerial, reconnaissance of specified border zones by joint Indo-Pak teams to ensure deployments were not taking place.
5. Current arrangement to ensure regular border meetings could be widened to routine visits by service chiefs . This has often been suggested but not found possible due to political exigencies. The irony is compounded here by the fact that retired Service Chiefs are active in Track Two exercises. Such exchanges of visits by military officials could be extended to allocation of seats in college of military instruction to allow greater reassurance being gained by the two military establishments[48].

Several further confidence building measures in the Indo-Pak context could be envisaged. Many have indeed been suggested in the "non-papers" exchanged by the two countries in January 1994[49]. The two non-papers presented by Pakistan on January 18 called for a plebiscite in Kashmir. The six "non papers" offered by India proposed ensuring of peace along the line of control in Kashmir, withdrawal from the Siachen Glacier, settlement of the boundary in the Sir Creek, resolving the Tulbul dispute in Kashmir, reviving the India - Pakistan joint commission and extending the agreement on non-attack of nuclear facilities to population and economic centers apart from a bilateral agreement not to be the first to use or threaten to use their nuclear "capability" against each other.

The limited applicability of CSBM's to the South Asian situation raises the question whether non-military CSBMs might prove more efficacious In contrast to the prophylactic character of military CSBMs, non-military CSBM's are designed to generate an atmosphere conducive to stability by softening the edges of mutual suspicions and enlarging the areas of cooperation between the adversarial states[50].

The linked nature of sub-continental policy makes it possible for inter-state cooperation to be premised on commercial, communications and environmental homogeneities. For example, the traditional directions of trade, was disrupted during the colonial period by linking the regional to the metropolitan economy. This process has been accentuated due to disruptions caused by political exigencies. Apropos harnessing the hydro-electric potential of the eastern Himalayan river water system has not proceeded because no bilateral / trilateral arrangements has been established between India, Bangladesh and Nepal. A huge economic penalty attaches to this intransigence emerging from the tangled politics of South Asia[51].

The Simla Agreement (1972) provided, inter alia, for establishing non-military CSBM's. One of its key provisions envisaged that two countries (India and Pakistan) would put an end to the conflict and confrontation that have hitherto marred their relations and work for the promotion of a friendly and harmonious relationship and the establishment of durable peace in the Subcontinent so that both countries may henceforth devote their resources and energies to the pressing task of advancing the welfare of their people.

In order to restore and normalise relations between the two countries step by step, it was agreed that:

1. Steps shall be taken to resume communications, postal, telegraphic, sea, land, including border posts and air links including over flights.
2. Appropriate steps shall be taken to promote travel facilities for the nationals of the other country.
3. Trade and cooperation in economic and other agreed fields will be resumed as far as possible.

4. Exchange in the fields of science and culture will be promoted.

These salubrious provisions provide a model for emplacing non-military CSBM's between South Asian countries. Pertinently, the South Asian Association for Regional Cooperation (SAARC) was established in 1985 to accelerate economic growth in the region by collective self-reliance. Several areas for cooperation have been identified. They include agriculture, telecommunication technological / scientific development, poverty alleviation, establishment of a food security reserve population control, environmental protection and so on. The creation of South Asian Preferential Trade Agreement (SAPTA) economic cooperation in the region has been ratified by all countries in the region permits the trade instrumentality being utilized to reduce tensions in the subcontinent. These measures could establish a web of non-military CSBM's in South Asia.

This list could be extended within the available matrix of Simla Agreement But priority needs to be accorded to four areas that are of prime significance to harmonizing the regional milieu in South Asia. These are:

1. First, the establishment of more convenient travel facilities between the South Asian countries. These are designed at present to discourage travel because of the extremely inconvenient travel schedules, and unavailability of sufficient air flights, trains and surface transport.
2. Second, visa requirements need to be relaxed to the largest extent possible. It is ironical that citizens belonging to South Asian countries are subject to different criteria for giving visas. The situation obtaining in the Indo-Pak context is that involved procedures, deliberate bureaucratic delays and unofficial quotas deter all but the most persistent of visa applicants. Successful visa applicants have to subject themselves to the indignity of reporting to the nearest police station on arrival and also when they depart. The official justification for the policy is the need to ensure reciprocity

in such matters. But the real intention behind this policy is clearly to discourage people to people contact between citizens of the two countries.

3. Third, the cessation of negative/hostile propaganda as a is urgently required by the South Asian countries. They contribute immensely to tense relations and to fomenting communal disturbance in the region. Again, this activity proceeds with official support because the electronic and visual media in South Asia remains largely under state control.

4. Fourth, considerable distortion and misrepresentation, continues in the textbooks used, particularly in India and Pakistan, despite the existence of an Indo-Pak agreement committing both countries to refrain from such misrepresentations.

Another significant non-military CSBM is the Lahore Declaration. This declaration is a landmark for peace and security of the two nations. The two countries have agreed that they -

1. Shall intensify their efforts to resolve all issues including the issue of Jammu and Kashmir.
2. Shall refrain from intervention and interference in each others internal affairs.
3. Shall intensify their composite and integrated dialogue process for an early and positive outcome of the agreed bilateral agenda.
4. Shall take immediate steps for reducing the risk of accidental or unauthorised use of nuclear weapons and discuss concepts and doctrines with a view to elaborating measures for confidence building in the nuclear and conventional fields aimed at prevention of conflict.
5. Reaffirm their commitment to the goals, and objectives of SAARC and to concert their efforts towards realisation of the SAARC vision for the year 2000 and beyond with a view to promoting the welfare of the peoples of South Asia and

to improve their quality of life through accelerated economic growth social progress and cultural development.

6. Reaffirm their condemnation of terrorism in all its forms and manifestations and their determination to combat this menace.

7. Shall promote and protect all human rights and fundamental freedoms.

Similarly the two countries will engage in discussions to conclude the argument on the prevention of war hostilities at sea, in order to ensure safety of navigation by navel vessels, and by aircraft belonging to the two sides of countries would also periodically review the implementation of existing CBMs as well as the existing links at operational levels like the hotline between the Director Generals of Military Operations, with these links fail-safe and secure.

Several types of useful Transparency Measures (TMs) can be envisaged given the situation between India and Pakistan. Among these (TMs), perhaps the most important is the publication of annual defense budgets that clearly spell out the allocations for various arms. If particular allocations, has been increased, it should be adequately highlighted, giving the reasons for the increase. This would remove all grounds for the misinterpretation by the adversaries.

Detailed coverage of parliamentary debate on defense in the national press could enhance openness. Increased awareness could also stimulate renewed thinking within and outside the government The publication of annual defense budgets and consequent detailed press coverage of parliamentary debates is a form of direct communication not only with the nation in question but also in other interested nations.

Information regarding the size, structure, weapons, cantonments, future inductions, purchases and movements of forces would be shared with both interested parties, both inside and outside the country. Extremely useful TM is the publication and circulation among interested parties of annual calendar exercises. This calendar could mention the area in which the exercises are to be held. Exercise could be prohibited in areas that are either too close to the border or viewed as extremely sensitive. In addition spelling out the objectives of a particular exercise in detail would be helpful. For instance, a particular exercise might be described as testing of a new terrain and new tactics, or as introducing new weapons, or a combination thereof.

An agreement to invite observers from an adversary state to witness military exercises could be extremely useful to further enhance openness. In 1989, when Pakistan undertook its military exercises, attaches from various embassies were invited including India. This was tended to confirm the non-hostile intention of Pakistani exercises.

All unscheduled movement of troops whether caused by internal crisis or an emergency on a border need to be notified as quickly as possible. A regularized pattern of notification tends to generate confidence in the openness of a country's policies.

Tests covering all aspects of sophisticated weaponary need to be announced publicly. Particular attention should be paid to tests of nuclear and missile technology. The nuclear weapon applications of missile technology and the fact that there are currently no effective defences against missiles make the development and testing of missiles a cause for significant concern in adversary countries.

Higher military training institutions should invite attendance and participation from perceived and known adversaries. Inviting an Indian participant to Pakistan's National Defense course or a Pakistani to a similar course in India would be a CBM that would be clearly indicate the course structure and objective. Joint courses could be organized at a regional level that would enable all the regional countries to explore the avenues of collective defense of the region[52].

A method of annual information exchange among interested states could be devised[53]. This could be done at two levels - either comprehensive defense books could be published indicating the existing strength of active and reserve forces, various weapons, defense productions and other aspects of defense preparendness, a regional or bilateral agreement could be signed in which countries agree to supply the desired information on demand. A comprehensive defense book could be published either by the individual country or by a regional organisation employing a commission of military experts from member states.

All arms procurement agreements including those containing transfer of technology could be made public. For example, arms sale transactions could be published in a UN register[54], which would enable each side to verify transactions when it is deemed necessary.

Exchange visits of high military officials and regular meetings of officers at lower levels could be encouraged. Regular meetings of military attaches with their counterparts in the host country would provide a useful channel of communications establishing a dialogue regarding security issues. To satisfy each other's inquisitive instinct and allay apprehensions a system inspections on demand could be introduced. Sometimes an inspection is required merely to satisfy the government highly developed sensitivities of governments and is not meant to cast doubt on the other country's explanation. An open skies treaty can be extremely useful in promoting openness of military forces and activities[55]. All conventional defense productions units could be opened for visits of officials from other countries including those of adversaries.

Advanced research regarding the prevention of nuclear accidents and the thorny problem of nuclear waste disposal could be made public. Alternatively collaborative joint programmes could be initiated aimed at preventing nuclear accidents and demising means for the safe disposal of nuclear waste[56].

Broadly speaking four sets of obstacles tend to hinder progress in this area and discourage constructive efforts at both individual and collective levels. These hindrances are –

1. Historical Problem,
2. Mutual Misperceptions
3. Domestic Developments and
4. Current Regional Disputes.

The cold war between India and Pakistan predates the British departure from the Indian subcontinent and can easily be traced back to colonial rule and to the rivalry between the Indian National Congress and the Muslim League. After Partition this rivalry involved into conflict following issues such as mass migration and refugee problems evacuee properties, water disputes, the division of financial and military assets and the problems of integration of princely states took their toll on Indo-Pakistani goodwill. The Kashmir dispute arose out of partition and continues to impede almost all normalization efforts. Both sides have repeatedly stressed without a resolution of the Kashmir issue, peace is an unlikely scene in South Asia.

Conflict and tension have also arisen in South Asia because of different perceptions and different images the protogonists have each other. Misperceptions tend to paint a totally different picture than that which actually exists. Sometimes these distorted perceptions are acquired because of lack of information. At other times misperceptions by leaders and decision makers are deliberate.

Perceptions or misperceptions need to be considered at two levels public and governmental. Perceptions tend to give substances to varying interpretations and misinterpretations. For example, Pakistan's sense of insecurity during the initial days of independence prompted it to enter into the western defense alliance system. India saw this as an attempt to challenge Indian authority in South Asia, because India had envisaged for itself a central role' not only in South Asia but also in Asia, and arrival of an out side equalizer could upset its entire design.

Domestic pressures and upheavals also tend to disrupt many constructive international processes and are known to have contributed substantially to major foreign policy shifts in most countries of the world. Governments commonly use external events to divert attention from pressing internal, political, economic, social and even security crises. Hostile external responses make it relatively easy to enhance internal cohesion by employing emotional and sentimental jargon. One does not have to look too deeply into the prevailing situations in India and Pakistan to see the existence of strong pressures generated by various internal crisis. India and Pakistani leaders have almost always exploited the others internal turmoil and tensions for their own advantage. Three types of situations have tended to develop most frequently: the periodic emergence of minority governments an incumbent government, unable to resolve an internal crisis that begins to rely too heavily on diversionary tactics, and the development of excessive influence by certain vested interests.

Among the ongoing disputes that are taking a continually heavy toll on bilateral relations are Kashmir, the Siachen Glacier, the Sir Creek, the Tulbul Plant, the Wular Lake Barrage and the nuclear weapons programmes on both sides of the border. India's nuclear programme is far more advanced and more comprehensive than Pakistan's. India has already tested a nuclear device, established a large fleet of bombers and secured the requisite missile technology and is now rushing to perfect long-range missiles and satellite capabilities. Although, the government of India has always stressed the peaceful intention of its nuclear programme, informed press reports have periodically suggested that India never abandoned its nuclear weapons programme. Pakistan on the other hand, while it has also proclaimed its nuclear programme, has recently acknowledged that it has acquired the technical capabilities to make nuclear devices.

CSBM's are emerging in South Asia since 1990's as a middle course between rising force and resolving fundamental issues. What is absent is a willingness to resolve fundamental issues such as the future and the Kashmir and reluctance to use force in nuclearized South Asia. India and Pakistan have now chosen bilateral CSBMs almost by default as their preferred approach to conflict resolution. By appropriately expanding the nascent network of bilateral CSBM's the three largest states of South Asia could probably improve their security, foster a climate of interstate relations, and perhaps, eventually may be willing to negotiate resolutions of the fundamental issues that divide them.

CSBM's are neither necessary as a basic for making progress in other areas nor sufficient to resolve the security problems of South Asia. Nonetheless, they can contribute to both. The Simla Agreement, although an existing mutual security pledge between India and Pakistan, should not be given much credence. Not only is it interpreted quite differently by the two countries, and it did not prevent major crisis in 1987, 1990 and recently 1999, but Pakistan also regards it as illegitimate, it having been forced to sign it after losing the 1971 war. The Indo-Pakistan agreement not to attack each other's declared nuclear facilities, and to refrain from obtaining chemical weapons, are likely to be more useful. Neither goes as far, however, as the Sino-Indian pledge that outstanding border issues would be solved only by peaceful means and in the meantime to respect the line of control. Although as a revisionist power, Pakistan should not be expected to agree easily to mutual pledge with India to refrain from the use or threat of use of force to settle outstanding issues. Such a mutual security pledge would probably provide as great an assurance as is possible in still-volatile South Asia. Of less but still considerable value, would be mutual pledges between India and Pakistan not to be the first to use nuclear weapons against the other. The reluctance of India and Pakistan to acknowledge fully their nuclear weapons capabilities need not be a significant impediment here. Diplomats in both countries are surely up to the task of finding a formulation of such a pledge that would not require either side to acknowledge what it prefers to leave ambiguous. Whether the nuclearization of India and Pakistan can be reversed or halted through joint support to the Nuclear-

Nonproliferation Treaty or by some other means of mutually eschewing nuclear weapons, or even whether their mutual security would be best served by this cause, are matters on which the opinions are different.

TMs can enhance deterrence and lengthen warning times of hostile intentions, thus enhancing security and reassuring potential enemies that the other is not preparing for war or coercive military action, thus enhancing confidence. Because of these dual functions, TM's might be most useful CSBMs. Some requirements now exist for prior notification of military exercises along the Indo-Pakistani borders and regular, although, limited, military to military contacts are required. These are all useful initial steps. A longer period for advanced notification, publication of an annual calendar of exercises, enlargement of the set of exercises requiring advanced notification and advanced notice of all troop movements would all be useful extensions of current agreements. Inviting observers to witness exercises and expanding military to military contacts through exchange visits of senior strategists and planners and cross attendance at military training institutions would further enhance transparency. So would further disclosure of military budgets, weapons inventories and purchases, force deployments and construction of militarily relevant infrastructure, especially by Pakistan. Open skies agreements, allowing reconnaissance overflights of each other's territory, would be an extremely useful transparency CSBM, but are unlikely to be agreed upon any time soon.

So long as mutual suspicions and the level of military activity at sea or along mutual borders and lines of actual control are high, agreements to manage dangerous and potentially military activities and accidents would be beneficial to all. Some beginnings have been made in the area of overflights, and accidental air intrusions between India and Pakistan. Also needed are naval agreements regulating activities by the growing Indian navies that might be regarded as hostile or threatening, agreement not to test missiles in the direction of another country and agreements to prevent and limit the consequences of nuclear accidents.

For crisis management, some hotline communications exists between ground force headquarters, and in some cases commanders, but not yet between air force headquarters or between senior political authorities. Moreover, communication is currently made in voice rather than text, which is less susceptible to misinterpretation and hasty judgment. The mechanisms now in place to prevent and mitigate crisis along the Sino-Indian line of control could productively be carried over to the Indo-Pakistan relationship. However, this is unlikely to happen until, if ever, both sides are willing to accept this line as a de facto international border, as India and China essentially have, pulling forces back from limiting the size of force deployments and the types of weapons allowed along the lines of control would also be highly valuable crisis management CSBM's. Some progress in these areas has been made between India and China, but not yet between India and Pakistan. As the existence of nuclear capability gradually infuses thinking about South Asian security, ways should be found to avoid any state from having an incentive to launch a preemptive attack. This implies that each country should assure the other that its nuclear assets are neither excessively vulnerable nor capable of independent initiative outside of political control. There is much room here for unilateral action. However, mutual agreements, through CSBMs might also be useful and feasible to a limited extent[57].

References:

1. Kashmir: The Real Big Hurdle, The Initial Phase: Partition of India, Indo-Pak, Wars, UNO Page, 114.
2. Sehgal Narender "Converted Kashmir", Utpal Publications.
3. The Challenge in Kashmir English translation of his famous Sanskrit epic "Rajtarangini" (composed 1150) available in Stain (1991).
4. Sharma K. Suresh and Usha Sharma (eds.) "Kashmir Through the Ages", Deep & Deep Publications.

5. Kashmir: The Real Big Hurdle, The initial Phase: Partition of India, Indo-Pak, Wars, UNO Page, 114.
6. Chaturshreni Ved Vati "Indo-US Relations" New Delhi, National Publishing House 1980 P. 135 and Sen Chanakya. "India and United states", Mainstream, Vol. 11 No.20 January 18, 1964, P.14.
7. US Department of State Bulletin. Vol. LIV April 25, 1966, P.669.
8. K Rossinger Lowerence "India and the United States: Political and Economic Relations, New York: Macmillan, 1950, P. 150.
9. The US principles include first a lasting political settlement must be an agreed settlement. Second, the Security Council will always welcome agreement of the parties which will settle the dispute which is consistent with the role of the Security Council to assist the parties in seeking to reach agreement Fourth, agreement most frequently is reached step by step through negotiations and involves an element of compromise. Finally, the Security Council should consider with care the views and recommendations of its representative and inform him the parties' views on the positions he has taken. See US Department of State Bullentin Vol. XXVIII, December 29, 1952, P.1028.
10. USIA Transcript: "Talbolt World net Dialogue on South Asia" Wireless File November 17, 1993.
11. Dr. Samar Mubarakmand, the Pakistan scientist in charge of Pakistan's nuclear tests in 1993, cited in the Gulf Today, May 19, 1999, Also see Pakistan's Time May 20, 1999.
12. Singh Jasjit "Pakistan's Fourth War for Kashmir", Asian Strategic Review 1998-99.
13. Usman Ali in Takkeer, June 10, 1999 cited in POT (Pakistan) June 21, 1999, P. 2143.
14. Krishnaswamy Sridhar "Pak Intrusion Was Planned Two Years Ago" The Hindu July 1999.
15. Dawn, June 17, 1999.
16. Alam Aroosa in Pakistan Observer June 16, 1999, cited in POT (Pakistan) July 2, 1999 p. 2295.
17. Gauhar Altaf, "Four Ways, One Assumptions" Nation, September 5, 1999.
18. According to the Pakistani newspaper, Takkeer (June 10,1999) Ali Usman stated, "In 1994 General Ziauddin finalised a plan to dislodge the Indian Army from Siachen. The most important part of the plan was to cut the India supply line to Siachen.

19. The Hindu, July 1, 1999.
20. Abbas Zaffar, "Whodunnit"? The Herald August 1999, P. 66.
21. Editorial, Friday Times July 30, August 5, 1999.
22. Journal of Peace Studies Vol. 6. Issue 3, May-June 1999, p.p. 3.
23. Srivastava, H.K. "The India-Pakistan Strategic Debate; The Hold off Approach" Strategic Studies Journal Vol. (1-2), Phase (1).
24. Kavie J. Lorne India's Quest for Security: Defence Policies 1947-65, Berkeley University of California Press 1967 pp. 27-28.
25. New York Times, May 13, 1998, P.A. 12.
26. Spector S. Leonard and Jaequeline R. Smith Nuclear Ambitions: The Spread of Nuclear Weapons 1989-90, Bounder Colo, West View: 1990, P. 64.
27. Recently desclassified US government documents provide fascinating details of the parleys, which could have led to India remaining non-nuclear. For a partial account of the negotiations for security guarantees, see, Battle Joyce, National security Archive Electronic Book No.6: India and Pakistan- On the Nuclear Threshold 1998.
23. For one account of Enterprise incident see Blechman, et al. Force Without War: 45 Armed Force as a Political Instrument, Washington. D.C.: The Brooking Institution pp. 175-223.
29. The perception in India of potential threats especially of coercion and blackmail intensified after President Richard Nixon (1911-) stated in 1985 that he had considered using nuclear weapons during the Indo-Pak war in 1971, although more in the context of China intervening (the reason why India had signed the treaty with the USSR). See Nixon Richard, Time Magazine, July 29, 1985.
30. Singh, Jasjit Frontline April 24, 1998. However the test certainly strengthens credibility for greater degree than other methods.
31. The roots of the policy of non-alignment can be traced back in India to at least 1939 when the leading Indian National Congress Party (at its session at Haripur) passed a resolution "India is resolved to maintain friendly and co-operative relation with all nations and avoid entanglements in military and similar alliances which tend to divide up the world into rival groups and thus endanger world peace".
32. Singh Jasjit "India's Nuclear Policy: A Perspective" Strategic Analysis Vol. XIII no VIII, November 1939, PP. 781-802.
33. Where technology was transferred from West European States and not from India.

34. For the text of Indian Nuclear Doctrine sec Observer of Business and Politics, August 20, 1999.
35. R. Chiddambaram, Chairman Atomic Energy Commission said in Mumbai see Times of India August 17, 1999.
36. See the text of D.R. Mankekar Memorial Lecture by George Fernandes, at India International Center, New Delhi on August 8, 1998.
37. New York Times, May 14, 1993.
38. The Times of India May, 14, 1993.
39. Ibid, June 23, 1993.
40. Cohen P. Stephen and Ganguly Sumit "India in Robert Chose, Emily Hill and Paul Kennedy (eds.). The Pivotal States: A New Framework for US Policy in the Developing World (New York: W. W. Norton 1997, P. 57).
41. Kamath P.M. "US-China Relations Under the Clinton Administration: Comprehensive Engagement or the Cold War Again?" Strategic Analysis Vol. 21 No. 5 August 1998.
42. Kamath P.M. "The US Role in South Asia since the End of the Cold War: From Pakistan to a Balance and a Pakistan Again", in Chaturvedi Arun and Lodha Sehgal (eds.) India's Foreign Policy and the Emerging World Order, Jaipur: Printwell Publishers, 1998 and Kamath P.M. "Indo-US Relations During the Clinton Administration: Upward Trends and Uphill Tasks Ahead", Strategic Analysis Vol. 21 No-11, February 1998.
43. Text of speech "Post Cold War-Weapons Spread Spurs Need for Arms Control", Publich Diplomacy Querry.
44. Dr. Alam Aftab Pakistan's Nuclear Development and Capability, Third Concept April-May 1998.
45. POT, Pakistan May 25, 1999.
46. Defence and Foreign Affairs Weekly, February 19-25, 1990, P.3.
47. The Nation, July 4, 1997.
48. A more comprehensive list is included in Malotts, " Report to Congress on Progress Towards Regional Non-proliferation in South Asia; US Department State April 1993.
49. Chari P.R. Strategic Studies Journal Vol. IX, P. 96-47.
50. For a factual account of the "non-papers" exchange process USIS official Text, Third Report to Congress: Update on Progress toward Regional Non-proliferation in South Asia, April 18, 1994, PP 8-10.

51. Chari P.R., Navnita Chadha and Maroof Raza Confidence Building Measures in South Asia, New Delhi: Centre for Policy Research January 1995, P.5.
52. Ahmar Moonis, "The Applicability of the Helsinki Model for the Task of Confidence Building and Conflict Resolution in the Indo-Pak Sub continent contemporary South Asia 1994" 3(3) esp. PP. 244-46.
53. Cheema Pervaiz. Iqbal, "Transparency Measures Mending Fences, Confidence and Security Building Measures in South Asia (ed) by Sumit Ganguly and Ted Greenwood, Delhi Oxford University Press, 1997.
54. Corden S. Pierce, Building and strengthening Confidence and Security in Asia", Disarmament Topical paper no. 10, New York: United Nations 1992, PP. 163-73.
55. Ruth Friedrich "Transparency and Confidence Building, Disarmament" Topical paper no-3 New York: United Nations, 1990, PP 63-65.
56. Jones Peter, "Open Skies: A New Era of Transparency", Arms Control Today, May 1992, PP 10-15. Also see "Open Skies Treaty", in US Department of State Dispatch March 30, 1992.
57. Cheema Pervaiz Iqbal, "Transparency Measures" Mending Fences, Confidence and Security Building Measures in South Asia (ed) by Sumit Ganguly and Ted Greenwood, Delhi Oxford University Press, 1997.
58. Ganguly Sumit and Ted Greenwood (eds.) Mending Fences Confidence and Security Building Measures in South Asia, Delhi Oxford University Press, 1997.

3

USA and Indo-Pak Relations Since 1990

Almost all the commentaries on any aspect of American foreign policy looks up on the USA as the only superpower in a "unipolar moment", the indispenseble nation, the one nation essential to world stability. Indeed however much they may disagree about the appropriate way for the United States to play its new role of unchallenged dominant power, government officials, opponents and pundits all share an image of the United States as a power without peer in the post cold war world.

USA: Catalysing Factor in South Asia

With end of the cold war the US assumed a greater role with great euphoria. The implications of this euphoria for the US South Asian dialogue can be seen in terms of three dilemmas: the dilemma of misguided expectations when the US is looked upon for aid, support and assistance due to its sheer dominance. Every country wants the US to solve its problems or at least to assist it in solving them often dislikes the method and substance characteristic of America's intervention". The second is the dilemma of misjudged power. According to Johnson "the dominant power has more influence-more capacity to act-than any other power but often has less capacity to work its will than people at home and abroad think it has and expects it to have, leading to the frustration of excessive expectation unfulfilled". The third is the dilemma of misplaced resources. Johnson explains that by virtue of its very dominance the dominant power (US) has interest that are world-wide but it is often difficult or impossible to identify threats to these interests, which will command consensus or mobilize resources. Reflecting these dilemmas American foreign policy debates have come to center round 'broad' models of American global engagements the 'hegemonist' and the 'militarist'[1].

Now the question arises, how important is South Asia to the United States? South Asia like all other major areas of the world is of vital importance to the United States and demands more attention. Though past contacts between the United States and South Asia were limited, this is a part of the world which is still open to the United States and with which meaningful contacts and co-operative policies are possible.

In the great issues of war and peace and therefore of human survival, the United States has been far less concerned with South Asia than with the former Soviet Union or with its NATO allies where the balance of world power presently rests. In the foreign policy concerns of the United States, namely survival, the development of effective deterrent power, the prevention of a nuclear war and the steady pursuit of the national interest during a period protected conflict South Asia does not have a determining place but even in these areas of vital concern, India the largest country of the non aligned movement and Pakistan, America's major Asian ally cannot be ignored.

The scenario of the South Asian security has remained grim over the last half decade. To a large extent the agonising historical past, the mutual mistrust, distorted perceptions and the uneasy relationship between India and Pakistan since 1947 are considered to be the root case of insecurity in South Asia.

However, on a smaller scale the power politics of the cold war era and the role-played by the US in the post cold war era can also be considered crucial for the prevailing situation of insecurity in South Asian.

Its own national interest, economic imperatives and global perspective have always guided the US foreign policy toward South Asia. In the post cold war era too the US is still in a position to aggravate or lessen or redeem a situation of insecurity in this region. Although the disintegration of the Soviet Union and end of the cold war has brought about drastic changes in the international relations, yet these changes have failed to execute any perceptible change in the relationships between India, Pakistan and the US. On one hand, Pakistan continues to be a constant and imminent threat to India's security, and on the other side the US decision to resume military aid to Pakistan after a gap of five years clearly shows Pakistan's important place in the global designs of the US in the post cold war. Why has the end of the cold war neither cooled US Pak relationship nor warmed up Indo-US relations is a question that tempts one to further probe this interesting scenario, because it also suggests that this relationship was not a part of the cold war power politics. The present equation of triangular relationship attempts to analyse the problem of peace and security in South Asia in the context of the new equation amongst India, Pakistan and the US in the post cold war world.

It is interesting to note that US policy has always exhibited a tilt in Pakistan's favour, which can also be cited as an important example of policy of opportunism in South Asia. As Thornton has written that "the 1971 help to Pakistan was not Pakistan because of specific US interest in South Asia but as a result of global concerns, super power politics and non-proliferation. When there is no such intervening factor, we must assume that the relatively low trend line is the normal level for the US-Pakistan relations"[12].

This tilt in favour of Pakistan can be explained in terms of the intensity of the expanding communist influence in South Asia. As and when the US saw this threat Pakistan gained far more importance than India for the USA. It was only due to this threat perception that Pakistan became a front line state to provide all types of assistance to the Afghan militants fighting against the Soviet occupation. During this period in its worry to curtail the communist threat in South Asia, the US not only supplied latest weaponry to Pakistan but also overlooked Pakistan's nuclear programme. In fact, Pakistan was initiated into nuclear technology with the knowledge and cooperation of the US itself, despite its great advocacy for nuclear non-proliferation. But with the Soviet withdrawal from Afghanistan in 1989 not only Pakistan's importance as a frontline state receded, but US pressures on Pakistan to cap its nuclear programme also increased, and economic and military aid to Pakistan was stopped because it had imported items related to reprocessing of nuclear fuel.

The US assistance to Pakistan was stopped in 1979, under the Symington and Glenn Amendments, by President Carter. But in order to meet the new challenges in the form of the Soviet occupation of Afghanistan the President was authorized to waive the provisions of this law and aid to Pakistan was resumed in 1982. The Pressler Law, which came into existence in 1982 was also not applied to Pakistan till 1989. This amendment stipulated an annual certification by the President that Pakistan did not posses a nuclear device[3].

Until 1989, the US Presidents annually signed the certificate regarding Pakistan not having nuclear know-how because Pakistan had an important place in the global designs of the USA. But after the Soviet withdrawal from Afghanistan, the US did not find any compulsion to give Pakistan a clean chit and in accordance to the clauses of the Pressler Amendment, the aid to Pakistan was totally stopped. Though in most of Pakistan's think tanks opinion the US attitude had been unfair, as it has largely ignored India's nuclear programme and always attempted to impose penalties on Pakistan's programme[4].

But from the Indian view point, the US policy of initially providing certificate that Pakistan does not possess a nuclear explosive device and thereafter refusing this certificate has lent a greater legitimacy and credibility to Pakistan's nuclear programme, and its purported success is being capable of manufacturing nuclear weapons[5].

The end of cold war provided with opportunities for the much needed changes in this triangular relationship. It was felt that in the absence of the irritants of the cold war era, India's non-alignment and close ties with the former USSR and United

States tilt and arms supplies to Pakistan, a new relationship would emerge between India, Pakistan and the United States. The US double standards were implicit in the fact that it remained reluctant to include India in the list of countries supporting terrorism despite New Delhi's well documented support to LTTE and other Tamil terrorist groups tearing Sri Lanka apart. At that time, even the Indian Press reports of Indian intelligence agencies having trained the LTTE activists, implicated in the assassination of Rajiv Gandhi could not convince Americans that India's track record in fomenting terrorism is far worse than that of all the countries on the US list of supporters of 'terrorism.

On the other hand, Pakistan's moral and diplomatic support to the Kashmiri Mujahideen, uprising against the Indian rule, has been termed as terrorism. Thus 1990-93 remained the crisis-ridden years, confined to crisis management in the shape of nuclear non-proliferation issues, terrorism, human rights and drug-trafficking[6].

The US realized that the Pressler Amendment was a blunt "instrument" that had not achieved policy goals but had proved counter-productive, and besides being a symbol of discriminatory treatment, was also a structural impediment to non-prolification in the region[7].

It is also believed to have acted as a disincentive to respond to any of the half a dozen non-prolification proposals that Pakistan has offered to India. The declaratory policy of the US 'balance' and 'even handedness', since 1995 could only have been termed as balanced if the US had removed all the discriminatory amendments against Pakistan. The Pressler sanctions have eroded Pakistan's conventional capability and have aggravated the military imbalance in the region. The inherent asymmetry in the conventional balance between Pakistan and India has been accentuated by the cut-off of all American military sales to Pakistan, whereas India has been extended economic assistance by the US and all types of military sales from Russia were also resumed after a short break.

The end of the cold war and the demise of the Soviet empire have generated security problems independent of the past US-Soviet rivalry. The proliferation of nuclear weapons and missile technology in the developing countries the emergence of regional hegemonus threatening the US regional and global interests and pressures of American public opinion to reduce the costs of global leadership and divert national resources for revival of their own domestic economy have created new imperatives and opportunities for redefining the US foreign policy both in theory and practice.

These changes have important implications for the US policy. It has effected US priorities in different regions. The nature and types of political, economic, scientific, technical and military developments need constant monitoring, which require enhanced technical and analytical capabilities. During the cold war the US policy of containment was essentially a single minded approach perceiving the predominant source of threat and seeking to meet it, whenever it jeoparalized vital interests of the US and its allies. However the post cold war political scenario has produced three paradigms of the US global policy imperatives, which played significant role in devising the policy of engagement and enlargement. The three paradigms are unipolarism, non-interventionism and multilateralism.

In newly emergent unipolar world the US is given preponderance in the world affairs with a half dozen other states having special strength that makes them salient, in certain cases (e.g. Japan is a global economic giant but weak in military and political prestige, Russia is militarily predominant in Eurasia but is crippled by political instability and economic weaknesses, unified Germany is preeminent in Europe but lacks the military capabilities of a global power, Britain and France wield certain diplomatic clout but rank below Germany in economic might and are also well behind the United States in military strength. China enjoys rapid economic growth but has to deal with uncertain political future and its armed forces are in dire need of modernization). The United States possesses a unique amalgam of political, economic, cultural and military clout that enables it to exercise unparalleled and multi dimensional influence throughout the world[8].

The concept of non-interventionism has replaced the old paradigm of 'isolationism'. Isolationism, in a strict sense, includes political, economic and military withdrawal from international affairs, but the concept of non-interventionism demands military disengagement only but not complete political detachment or economic autarky[9].

In such a scenario the use of the US armed forces for other purposes (countering regional aggression, supporting peacekeeping and humanitarian missions) almost always unwarranted, is dangerous, costly and futile, as only the market forces can provide much needed economic security[10].

India, born in an atmosphere of cold war, yet a peace-loving country, wanted to maintain friendly relations with every other country of the world. It adopted the policy of peace, non-alignment and co-existence, because it believed that if it kept away from rival powers it would be left in peace which was imperative for its all over development.

Nuclear Weapons – India – US

India has been a consistent opponent of the nuclear weapons ever since her independence. In fact, even before India gained independence, the Indian leaders expressed their shock over the dropping of the bombs at Hiroshima and Nagasaki, which resulted in enormous loss of life and property. After independence, India from every possible platform carried out a crusade against nuclear weapons, and tried to wean the nation away from the path of nuclear armaments. Jawaharlal Nehru, the first Prime Minister of India, and in charge of the Department of Atomic Energy stated on more than one occasions that India had nothing to do with the atom bomb, and she would like to use nuclear energy for peaceful purposes only, for example while inaugurating India's nuclear Reactor Apsara at Trombay in January 1957, he said.

"No man can prophesy the future. But I should like to say on behalf of my government and I think I can say with some assurance on behalf of any future Government of India, that whatever might happen, whatever the circumstances, we shall never use this atomic energy for evil purposes. There is no condition attached, to this assurance because once a condition is attached, the value of such an assurance does not go very far"[11].

India has consistently favoured the idea of use of nuclear energy for peaceful purposes because it was a vast source of power and could help in the development of the country. Jawahar Lal Nehru said in the Lok Sabha in 1954:

"The use of a atomic energy for peaceful purposes is far more important for a country like India, that is to say in a country whose power resources are limited than for a country like France, an industrially advanced country...... . It is important for a power starved or power-hungry country like India or most of the countries in Asia and Africa"[12].

India ultimately exploded an underground nuclear test device on May 18, 1974 at Pokhran, primarily with a view to find ways of using underground explosions for constructive purposes. The explosions was in keeping with the declared policy of India, and represented the resolve of the country to develop its indigenous resources of energy for the benefits of people through its own efforts.

Indian nuclear policy and disarmament diplomacy worked in tandem from early days. Jawahar Lal Nehru's appeal for nuclear tests moratorium in 1954 was designed as a disarmament measures. There were only three nuclear weapons powers and the two super powers had just conducted their first thermonuclear tests. The six Nation Initiative was also despised. India tried its best to keep the world nuclear free, and right after its independence, it had started sincere efforts in this direction. But these efforts were not welcomed in the then prevailing policies of cold war.

"No country in the world agonized over acquiring nuclear weapons for as long as India did or as much public debate. The

US, Soviet Union, Britain and China made their decision in secret without any debate. France had a very short debate among the non-nuclear weapon states, Isreal took the nuclear plunge in utmost secrecy and Pakistan too took the first step in secrecy in 1972 a little in defiance of the Indian decision[13].

Yet despite all the agreements for and against the exercise of the nuclear option, the Indian debate, unlike elsewhere, was largely on ethical grounds. Only a very small minority engaged the issue on considerations of international power politics or arms control. After the Pokhran II explosions, Prime Minister Atal Bihari Vajpayee gave a new slogan to the nation which was "Jai Vigyan". He said-

"This is recognition of the major role science and technology are playing in shaping our existence"[14].

The Prime Minister said:

> "While kisan feeds us and jawan protects us, science determines, how we are to live? It is India's scientific achievement that the nuclear blasts of May 11 and 13, 1998. There is a great euphioria in the country. Our scientists could successfully conduct those tests. I think we can be justifiably pleased that the scientists could demonstrate India's nuclear capability".

India carried out three and two nuclear explosions on 11 and 13 May 1998 respectively, leaving the whole world stunned. The heat and dust at the explosions site might have subsided by now, but in world politics it had become essential in the prevailing circumstances where India faces great threat to its security from the nuclear capability of China as well as Pakistan[15].

Nuclear Disarmament and Expectations from India:

Since 1947, every Indian government has been trying to face the challenge of protecting is border from North, East, West and South. While the decision of conducting nuclear tests has been commended by some doom has been predicted by others recommending severe punitive measures. While China holds India responsible for 'escalating nuclear arms race' in the erstwhile peaceful South Asia, Pakistan is all the more strident about it. It not only invoked international sanctions against India, but forged a simultaneous nuke programme of its own by conducting five nuclear tests in Changai Hills on 28th May[16].

The decision of the Indian Government has opened up a new debate in triangular relationship between India, Pakistan, and the US. The tests conducted by India and Pakistan stunned the world in general and the US in particular. The reactive and negative response from the West led by US was neither unexpected, nor surprising. The nuclear explosions in South Asia have dealt a severe blow to nuclear nonproliferation efforts, which top the US global security agenda in the post Cold War era.

India's reluctance and the US insistence on signing the NPT, CTBT or some other regional nuclear non-proliferation arrangement is not a new problem, but existed from the beginning of the NPT. In the past, especially after India's nuclear explosion in 1974 and 1998, the US has pressurized New Delhi on more than one occasion and in a number of ways to sign the treaties. Having realised that India can neither be persuaded nor pressurized to sign the treaties, the US has been suggesting ways other than the NPT to entrap India into is nuclear non-proliferation objectives. In the early 90s the US helped make Latin America, the Pacific and South Africa nuclear free zones. In 1991, India dismissed a proposal routed through Pakistan regarding a five nations conference for denuclearisation of South Asia. After assuming office, President Clinton has assumed a more activist role in arms control. Now the US is paying attention to South Asia because it perceives this region as the most likely theatre for a good diplomatic relations in the near future. American's objective is "first capping, then reducing, and eventually eliminating weapons of mass destruction from South Asia[17] said Strobe Talbott, US Deputy Secretary of State.

The principal concern of Clinton Administration is to prevent nuclear proliferation in South Asia, and to promote this objective it is eager to enlist India's support. India's serious reservations in this matter are well known to the USA, and any discussion on nuclear non-proliferation issue would require long and persuasive parleys. India has repeatedly made it known that while it stood committed to peaceful use of atomic energy,, it would not sign the NPT in favour of nuclear nations which will retain their nuclear arsenal while the non-nuclear nations will be debarred from having theirs.

One of the objectives of the US anti Indian posture on Kashmir and arming Pakistan during first years of Clinton Administration aimed at pressurizing India to give up its nuclear options. On their part nuclear haves have not placed their own nuclear arsenals on the agenda of non-proliferation and elimination as enjoined upon by Article 6 of the NPT, so as to retain the monopoly of coercive power.

The Bush-Baker South Asian policies also have nuclear aspects. They were interested in India signing the treaties, but at no stage India was subjected to pressures. On the contrary, the State Department had conclusive evidence regarding the Pakistani bomb and its adverse affects on the US interests. Ultimately the Pressler Amendment was applied against it to stop all aid and weapon supplies. The Clinton Administration, on the other hand, tried to persuade the Congress to roll back its harshness or agree to one time waiver to Pressler Amendments despite off and on statements by Pakistani officials that it has made a nuclear weapon and acquired missiles from China.

After the end of the cold war, the US is in great urgency to bring India and Pakistan into non-proliferation net, owing to several factors and developments. These are:

(i) The US intention to dominate in the post cold war unipolar world can only be realized by blocking emerging regional powers from developing nuclear weapons capability.

(ii) The US concern that South Asia does not export nuclear and missile capability to Iran, the Gulf and South West Asian countries. This development will not enhance the power of India and Pakistan but also go against the key strategic interests of the US i.e. the oil resources of the region.

(iii) The U.S. concern at India's rapid development in the nuclear and missile field, which has given the latter a degree of self-sufficiency. India has crossed important thresholds and acquired extra-ordinary range of capabilities in nuclear technology. It has successfully developed indigenous sophisticated technology to sustain the critical nuclear chain, fuels of various kinds, sufficient heavy waters reactors of varying and military use and reprocessing facilities capable of making weapons-grade plutonium from spent oil.

(iv) South Asia, that has witnessed four wars between India and Pakistan, is that most likely area of the world to explode and wage a nuclear war in the coming years. According to American experts, both India and Pakistan will be able to deploy nuclear weapons and they are developing ballistic missiles that could carry the weapons to selected targets.

Although the Clinton Administration claimed even-handedness in offering this non-proliferation regime to both India and Pakistan, it appears to be largely eager to revive its political co-operation with Pakistan. The US arms industry and the Pentagon are particularly interested in an early nuclear deal that would allow arms sales to Pakistan and reactivate the existing passive strategic nexus between Washington and Islamabad. Naturally India had to be worried about this coming closer of America and Pakistan given the recent American diplomatic activism on Kashmir, and Pakistan's propaganda on human rights and encouragement to terrorism. It is rightly apprehended that the prime objective of the American non-proliferation initiative appears to be to trap India into a regional nuclear arrangement that would let Pakistan off the Pressler hook[18].

Lee Hamilton, Chairman of the House Foreign Relations Committee of the US Congress, has stated that the US had -

"Largely ignored India's nuclear programme in recent years, while imposing substantial penalties on Pakistan's programme"[19].

Indirectly, he was suggesting that India should also be penalized equally for its nuclear programme.

During her visit to New Delhi in March 1994, Robin Raphel denied there was any pro-Pakistani tilt in the US policy on South Asia, and claimed the proposal to sell a batch of F-16 aircraft to Pakistan in exchange for a major, nuclear non-proliferation concession from Pakistan would enhance security in the region. She said United States pursued strong bilateral ties with both India and Pakistan, and this no tilt policy was in the interest of both countries[20].

The new American move to promote nuclear non-proliferation in South Asia aims at getting India and Pakistan to agree to cap their nuclear programmes, and accept international inspection of their nuclear production facilities. But, according to critics there is nothing new in this approach. All earlier initiatives to bring about bilateral regional accords on nuclear free zone had proved unsuccessful. The move is nothing more than old wine in new bottles. It may be a design to overcome strong Congressional resistance to the Administration earlier attempt to repeal the Pressler Amendment and supply F-16 combat aircraft to Pakistan. Originally, the Administration's had sought to oblige the Pakistani military establishment in return for the latter's programme. As the proposal did not succeed, Washington then came up with the idea of trapping India in capping its nuclear programme. This shows that there is not so much an eagerness to promote nuclear non proliferation, as is an overriding need to fulfill Pakistan's ambition to get hold of the sophisticated aircraft as soon as possible[21].

The effectiveness of verifiable capping of nuclear installations is also doubtful as the International Atomic Energy Agency remained unaware of Iraq's nuclear programme although it was a signatory to the NPT. Verification mechanism also proved futile in the case of North Korea, which too is a party to NPT. It will be in the fitness of things if the NPT review conference (1995) includes in its agenda credible verification of full compliance with nuclear obligations. From the moves of the Clinton Administration it would seem that as in the case of the nuclear non-proliferation treaty in the proposed fissile material cut-off convention too, there would also be categories of nations. Some will cut-off production but would be allowed to retain their past production of fissile material, and others would have to roll-back and then eliminate their production. India is clearly seen by the US in the later category, whereas Pakistan in the former.

Thus even among the category of the nuclear sudras, some like Pakistan would be more equal than others. When US deputy Secretary of State, Strobe Talbott came to New Delhi in April. 1994, disagreement persisted even on the question of nuclear non-proliferation. He stuck to the American stand that India should sign the treaty and the latter steadfastly refused to do so in its present form, on the ground that it was discriminatory by nature. The real problem in his view was the nuclear issue and production of fissile material, which posed grave danger to all humanity. That was the reason why the US government was pursuing the NPT issue vigorsouly in all available forums, bilateral talks or multilateral consultations.

India's contention that the logical inconsistency of the major powers keeping their vast nuclear arsenals while preaching abstinence to it and others in Asia, is not palatable to the US and other Western nations[22]. India does not see the nuclear issues from South Asia or regional perspective, and questions the need for countries like the USA, Britain and France using the NPT to apply a double standard on the issue - a double standard by which they keep the nuclear bombs they have, but try to stop them from reaching the developing third World.

India fails to understand why the nuclear powers hesitate to limit their own nuclear stockpiles and why they don't pledge to eliminate the stockpiles altogether and make the planet earth free from nuclear weapons.

The US has also continuously followed double standards in its non-proliferation policy. It has always opposed a comprehensive test ban treaty, and turned a blind eye to Isreal's nuclear weapons programme. It has never scolded China for clandestinely helping Pakistan develop its nuclear capability or sell it missiles. Moreover, the US over looked Pakistan's setting up of facilities to make nuclear bombs in the 80s.

During the past two decades or so, the nuclear powers have conducted hundreds of underground test explosions while delivering sermons to the world about the dangers from atomic weapons. India finds NPT as well as US's non-proliferation policy uneven, unequal and discriminatory. The new American proposals on nuclear nonproliferation run contrary to the fundamentals of India's nuclear policy. Accepting implies a regime of inspections, test bans and virtual end of fissile material production and missiles programme. For any Indian government it will be very difficult to agree to these prospects. Things have not moved towards a complete elimination of nuclear weapons as envisaged by Rajiv Gandhi Plan (1988) even after end of the cold war. Not only have the nuclear weapons states remained silent on the subject of the universal elimination of nuclear weapons, but they have also not taken any concrete steps in reducing their own nuclear weapons. On the other hand, countries like India have come under pressure to take steps to reassure the world that they will not make nuclear weapons despite India's voluntary restraint in this respect. Vinod points out, "the US policy of exerting pressure on India over the nuclear matter has turned out to be ineffective, if not counter productive, from the view point of promoting cooperation and understanding between the US and India"[23].

The US and the world should not forget that India has chosen the responsible policy of merely retaining, but not exercising the nuclear option. Unlike other nations, which depend on alliances for their security, India is a self-professedly non-aligned country which must ensure its own in a world or a region, which is neither free from conflicts nor from wars.

Nuclear Weapons—Pakistan—USA

In the past, Pakistan's ego, inflated by US military and economic aid, had influenced its judgement that only culminated in failure to wrest Kashmir away from India by force. US infused sense of parity had also fuelled its ambitions of becoming a South Asian power in direct rivalry with India. But in all these efforts, success alluded it invariably. The most significant thing that emerged from all this is the fact that it was the uppish Pakistani army that for the first time realized its limitations. The answer as to why Pakistan took to nuclear path lies in its own perceptions of its weakness manifested in repeated failures to achieve its objective vis-a-vis India.

During Vice-President Nixon's visit to Karachi in December, 1952, General Ayub Khan briefed him that Soviet Union would use "India as a cats paw". Nixon on the conclusion of his Karachi visit, declared on Radio Pakistan: "A strong independent Pakistan is an asset to the free world"[24], indicating a very clear, definite and lasting understanding between the two countries, USA and Pakistan. Bilal Hushmi in his lead article "Dragon Seed: Military in the state", penetratingly by elaborated: 'While the Pentagon and the representatives of Pakistan armed forces were engaged in expanding the small scale programme of 1952, the selective mass media in US was actively promoting favourable public opinion regarding possible benefits to US of the forthcoming defence alliance with Pakistan and to achieve the success of this promotion exercise, played down India's role in International affairs[25]'.

The first US-Pak defence treaty was signed at Karachi on May 19, 1954. Pakistan also became member of a number of US sponsored multilateral treaties like the South East Asia Treaty Organization, on September 5, 1954. Numerous other treaties were signed between Pak-US, which overwhelmed every aspect of the institutional Fabric of society[26]. Pakistan's first objective was to become a strong nation and overcome her deficiencies as compared with her far bigger neighbour India. To accomplish, this, Pakistan needed friends who would be able to give her economic, military help and prestige.

Becoming part of the prestigious nuclear fraternity was, therefore viewed by Pakistan as the only alternative 'that could nuetralize India. Soon the bomb began to play its role in Indo-Pak security equations. Development of number weapons after' 71 thus became its obsessive objective. For wider acceptence, emotive reasons and garnering Arabic world's financial resources, Bhutto called it an 'Islamic Bomb' and a common heritage. Notwith-standing the devious methods employed, an exclusive control of the Army, Bhutto's vision of wooing the Chinese successfully at a time when Pakistan was actively aligned with the West at the height of the cold war proved significant. China helped Pakistan at a time of its dire necessity by supplying it a proven design of the 'Bomb' that did not even require a field test.

This was a momentous gift that changed the very calculus of Indo-Pak relations. The Indo-centric policies of Pakistan made it a pliable ally of the USA, which saw in it a great strategic advantage vis-a-vis erstwhile Soviet Union and West Asia. Pakistan was ever ready to proclaim itself a "front line state" as long as it enabled it to pursue its own objectives, complying to the US dictates. Prime Minister Benazir Bhutto proclaimed in April 1995, at the joint press conference with President Clinton in Washington, that Pakistan was a "moderate, democratic and Islamic country that is strategically located at the trijunction of South Asia, Central Asia and the Gulf, a region of both political volatility and economic opportunity". This is an extraordinary and ludicrous attempt to sell the country for a small gain. If a theocratic state that practices Islamic fundamentalism, religious apartheid on minorities and non Sunni Muslims, and fuels terrorism not only in India but in other parts of the world also, can be declared a moderate state by the US, there could be nothing more absurd and perverse. The manner in which Pressler law has been bypassed by Hank Brown amendment in order to clear transfer of arms to Pakistan, shows US willingness to stoop down and compromise its own laws and principles on non-proliferation. In fact, when it comes to the US strategic interest, it is immaterial if its decisions are tantamount to arming a belligerent state that is advanced on destablishing the region. Ignoring India's security concerns and giving a big blow to stability in South Asia, to appease Pakistan, shows US duplicity at its worst. It would not only legitimise Pakistan's nuclear weapons but also enable it to upgrade its ability to deliver these.

This explains US renewed interest in Pakistan after a gap, and its willingness to compromise its principles. Interestingly, even earlier having invoked the Symington Amendment in 1979, withholding all aid to Pakistan in reaction to its nuclear programmes, USA dropped all its objectives suddenly for securing Pakistan's help in fighting the Soviets in Afghanistan. This time, the USA compromised its earlier stand of rolling back and then 'verifiable' cap, by declaring Pakistan a moderate Islamic state.

In the contemporary world political order, the US will have to adopt a more prudent South Asia policy as after having conducted main nuclear tests, both India and Pakistan are clamouring for a greater and more effective role. In world politics and if the US wants to maintain an effective procedure in this region of strategic political and economic importance, it has to achieve a fine balance in its South Asia policy and that too as fast as possible.

References

1. Johnson Glen M. "America at the Millennium, The Dilemmas of Dominance" Discourse In Trust - US - South Asia Relations (ed.) Kausar J. Azam South Asia Publishers 1997.
2. Thornton P. Thomas: The New Phase in US-Pakistani Relations Foreign Affairs Summer 1989, p. 154.

3. Chari R.P. "Indo-Pak Nuclear Stand Off. The Role of the United States Manohar Publications, New Delhi, 195, pp. 72-73.
4. General Beg Aslam Mirza: 'Pakistan's Nuclear Programme: A National Security Perspective In Nuclear Rivalry and International Order' ed. by Gielstad John and Njosstad Olan, Sage Publications New Delhi.
5. Lodhi Maleeha, Defining Moment in Pak-US Relations. The News, April 4, 1995.
6. Perry William, US Defence Secretary acknowledged in a speech to Foreign Policy Association New York, January 1994.
7. Huntington P. Samuel, "Americas Changing Strategic Interests", Survival, January/February 1991, p.6.
8. Carpenter, Galen Ted. "A Search for Alliances after the cold war", Washington D.C. Cato Institute 1992, p. 1839, See also Bandow Doug, "Keeping the Troops and the Money Home", Current History Jan 1994, p. 13.
9. Kohout J. John 111 et. al., "Alternatives Grand Strategy : Options for the United States" Comparative Strategy vol. 14 No.4 October-December 1994, pp. 384-85.
10. Khanna, V.N. "Foreign Policy of India", Vikas New Delhi 1997, p. 47.
11. Mahajan, V.D. "International Relations", p. 701.
12. Subramanyam B., Times of India, New Delhi, May 22, 1998.
13. Ibid.
14. Narlikar V.J. Times of India, New Delhi, June 22, 1998.
15. Dibaker "Politics India" Vimot, New Delhi, July 17, 1998, p. 17.
16. Gupta Rakesh, Mainstream Perspective New Delhi Vol. XXXVI No.21 May, 16, 1998, p. 3.
17. India Today, New Delhi April 50,1994, p. 45.
18. Raja Mohan C. "A Tempting Trap", The US Initiative on a Nuclear Freeze, Frontline (Madras) April 22, 1999, p. 121.
19. Indian Express (Chandigarh) May 1, 1994. p. 4.
20. Ibid March 26, 1994, p. 1.
21. Ibid, Editorial, p. 6.
22. US Latest Initiative 16, p. 34.
25. Vinod J.M n. IV., p. 245.

24. Rose Leo and Hussain A. Noor, "United States. Pakistan Forum: Relations with Major Powers 1987, p. 3.
25. Hushmi Bilal: "Dragon Seed: Military in the State; "Published in Pakistan and Roots of Dictatorship", 1983 p. 156, ed. By Gardesi and Rashid Malik.
26. Rashid Jamil and Gardesi, "Pakistan and Roots of Dictatorship", 1983, p. 158.

4

US Policies and Peace Prospects in South Asia Since 1990

India and Pakistan have a history of unresolved conflicts, wars and successful and unsuccessful peace processes. Deep-rooted suspicions, mutual distrust and antagonism continue to bedevil Indo-Pakistani relations even after the passage of nearly five decades. Despite the fact that economic and political development in South Asia has reached a stage where one might begin to contemplate with hope and optimism, the prospects of a normal neighbourly relationship, the conflicting interpretations of normalcy and priorities seem to be taking a continually heavy toll on the security and mutual confidence of the two countries. Although, both countries realize the need for normalcy, economic cooperation and regional stability acutely, they often make only minor concessions in peripheral areas. At the declaratory level, most leaders of the region have repeatedly asserted their desire to work for peace, but at the practical level any such effort has been viewed with suspicion and cynicism. With the departure of the cold war and the augured emergence of the "new world order", countries are however seriously looking for ways to implement the process that effectively reduced regional tension.

Conceptualising Peace

A peace process is a mechanism of negotiations where the parties involved attempt to avoid war or a war like situation, and wish to settle conflicts peacefully by using techniques such as diplomacy, bargaining, secret negotiations, trade off and mediation. Peace is considered as an end in itself and such techniques are used to achieve that end. A peace process is an exercise where groups or countries with conflicting interests seek to avoid further confrontation through negotiations.

Conflicts threatening regional or international peace and security require their peaceful management and resolution. However in order to launch a viable peace process,it is essential that the parties involved should have substantial political will and determination, and should be above suspicion to manage disputes through dialogue. Hence a peace process should largely be indigenous in nature with possible external assistance if desired by the parties concerned.

There are three important elements of a peace process: people, government and international community. Sometimes people may influence the course of events, and force the governments and the international community to launch a peace-process. This may happen by mobilizing people under peace groups, or the worsening of domestic conditions. Many times governments can change things and contribute to the peace process. The international community also has the power to influence things in a peace process, provided it has an interest in the particular situation. For a successful peace process it is essential that at least people and government should have a strong yearning for peace. Support from the international community is considered a plus point for any peace process. Since the attitude of the governments of India and Pakistan is not supportive for a peace process the international community cannot do much. If people of the two countries assert their positions for peaceful resolution of disputes, then in that situation the international community can play its role and compel the governments in New Delhi and Islamabad to launch a peace process.

A peace process may be divided into various levels, in case of India and Pakistan the Kashmir dispute could be called the core of peace process between the two countries, followed by other peace processes in Siachen, the nuclear issue and Wullar

Barrage. For the smooth sailing of a peace process, it is essential that the parties involved should keep a balance among different levels of the process. Sometimes, the groups involved in a peace process decide to freeze the core issue, and focus on less intractable problems.

In the backdrop of goodwill and euphoria generated between India and Pakistan through peace initiatives over the last more than ten years culminating in bilateral secretary level talk, the recent developments in the region indicate that road to peace is rather jagged.

The resolution of a conflict is somewhat an ideal goal in a peace process. While the participants in the process may have an idealized vision of a quick road to peace, in reality they need to aspire to a step-by-step management of the conflict. A peace process needs to send a clear message to the world that its participants have serious intentions to resolve their conflicts. They must also show that they realize the risk of derailing the peace process through politics of confrontation and understand the benefits if they move in the direction of peace building.

Perceptions of personalities involved in a peace-process play a key role for the success or a failure of any initiative. Sometimes, personalities involved in a peace-process start negotiations with deep-rooted suspicions, but eventually develop an objective and less parochial approach to the management of the conflict.

US Interest and Future of Peace in South Asia

The US nuclear policy has been majestically structured on the premise of two-fold objectives: preventing regional states from emerging as new centers of threat/force by slowing down the spread of nuclear weapons, and to develop non-military mechanism including diplomatic means, for the nuclear crisis management. The key factor that shapes and articulates the US policy is safeguarding its core national interests - security, economic and technological predominance, and also maintaining its liberal democratic and cultural values. With the end of the cold war the US has shown a marked interest in nuclear non-proliferation and has placed emphasis on strengthening global non-proliferation regimes and increasing its scope for action in defence of its supportive regimes. Such actions include increased transparency, intrusive inspections sanctions and even military action if necessary.

Today, when long lasting holdouts like China and France have finally come into NPT's fold, countries like Argentina, Brazil and South Africa have renounced their nuclear option, and North Korea has been virtually denied the right to invoke the withdrawal provisions, cCountries like India, Pakistan and Israel have emerged as the foremost targets of non-proliferation.

The US non-proliferation has evolved through four main stages: the post war security policy that was based on monopolistic control by the United States, the liberal policy ushered in through the "Atoms for Peace" policy of President Eisenhower; the policy of control through the NPT and creation of supplier policy following the challenges posed to NPT[1].

In the US nuclear policy of "Atoms for Peace Program", through signing and advocacy of the NPT, it tried for enactment of the Nuclear Non-Proliferation Act (NNPA-1978) and various other arms export control legislation. The common theme running through all administrations, has been the promotion of nuclear non-proliferation while they have been single mindedly concentrating their efforts on preventing horizontal nuclear proliferation in conjunction and cooperation with the former Soviet Union, they did little to prevent vertical proliferation. Not only that, the US kept its eyes closed on nuclear programs of some countries like Pakistan and Israel, where its national interests were at stake.

Nuclear nonproliferation as a part of its global non-proliferation policy. The United States has long advocated nuclear disarmament for South Asia. Its efforts to curb the spread of the bombs rest, on the premise that new nuclear systems will lead to instability as more is always seen as worse. Although Washington has shifted its strategies and tactics of controlling the bomb's spread globally[2], the administration's "Report to Congress Progress Toward Regional Non Proliferation in South Asia": April 1993, specifies that the US objectives is, "first to cap, then over time reduce, and finally eliminate the possession of weapons of mass destruction and their means of delivery"[3].

In regard to South Asia, one of the cardinal principles of the US foreign policy during the past few decades has been to deter the acquisition of nuclear weapons by India and Pakistan, and it has made non-proliferation a central issue in its bilateral relations with them. Since 1974, successive US administrations have pushed for restraint by both countries, utilizing a range of policy tools including diplomatic pressure, withholding of cooperation, embargoes on the export of nuclear technology and the leverage of US assistance and arms sales. Infact, the US has sought to oppose proliferation in South Asia through all means available at its disposal. Its goal has been to inhibit the development or acquisition of such systems, as well as to prevent their use to threaten others.

To achieve this goal (nuclear non-proliferation), the United States resorted to a range of policy instruments. According to Peter Galbraith, these instruments are:

i. An intensive effort to stop the acquisition by South Asian countries of the technology, equipment and fissile material for nuclear weapons. This involved consultations and cooperation with and the outright jawboning of other nuclear weapons programmes.

ii. The threat of, or actual use of, sanctions to discourage India and Pakistan from proceeding with nuclear weapons programme. Implemented sanctions have included the cut off of the United State's economic and military assistance and termination of supply of nuclear material.

iii. The use of incentives to encourage India and Pakistan to remain non-nuclear. So far these incentives have consisted of United States economic and military assistance.

iv. The offer of reliable supplies of nuclear material equipment and technology of the recipient country would accept full scope IAEA safeguards[4].

A historical shift in US policy towards South Asia was indicated during Talbott's visit to India when it decided to deal separately and on bilateral basis with India and Pakistan on nuclear issue. America reached a dead end in dealing with India and Pakistan together on nuclear issue, as India's stand always became a veto. So they are working to delink the two, and deal with them separately. Under new South Asia policy, the first major step is an attempt to cap the Pakistani nuclear weapons programme. In accordance with this ,Talbott asked Pakistan to examine the F-16s for capping proposal on its merits, and not bring India in the picture, as it were. Moreover, the nuclear issue was delinked from the resolution of the dispute between the two countries[5].

The US believed that the nuclear problem should be solved regionally and it was not proper to link the problem of one region with another.

Main features of American initiative on non-proliferation in South Asia are:

i. To ask Pakistan to accept a verifiable cap on its future nuclear programme. It will involve some kind of international inspection of the entire nuclear programme of Pakistan. US claims that it will stop Pakistan from producing additional nuclear weapons from the material it possesses.

ii. To ask India to accept a similar arrangements to halt its production of nuclear material for weapons purpose. This will bind India and place all its nuclear facilities under international safeguards.

iii. To convince India and Pakistan to join a multilateral conference on regional security that will include the five permanent members of the UN Security Council, and probably Japan and Germany as well. To make this scheme acceptable to Islamabad and New Delhi, Washington is offering incentives to both the countries-F-16 aircraft to Pakistan in exchange for a "major" nuclear non-proliferation concession from Pakistan, as it would enhance security in the region[6].

The US non-proliferation interests fall into or touch three different areas. According to Prof. Stephen P. Cohen these are:

i. There are purely nuclear related concerns, these include slowing down or controlling regional military nuclear programmes by stemming or stopping the flow of nuclear materials and technology to India and Pakistan, ensuring that they do not aid other states with their nuclear military programmes; seeing to it that the South Asian example of creeping proliferation is not emulated or admired elsewhere.

ii. There are two American strategic / global interests associated with regional proliferation. One is containment of Soviet influence in South Asia. It is important to ensure that if regional proliferation occurs it will not destabilize what will already be a very complicated global order.

iii. There are a number of regional American interests at stake. American policy since 1947 has favoured the emergence of a stable and cooperative South Asian Regional system based upon Indo-Pak cooperation so that all regional states might better solve their pressing economic and development problems[7] better.

These steps could include providing more transparency or more information on the production of fissile material and even placing it under some kind of monitoring. The US and Russia may also place 15-20 of bomb grade fissile materials under IAEA safeguard in near future. The US and Russia, it must be pointed out, no longer make fissile material because they have an enormous surplus of it[8].

The US also seeks to inhibit the export of nuclear weapon related equipment and technology from other countries to India and Pakistan. The US Under Secretary of State for International Security Affairs, Lynn Davis, while testifying before a Congressional Committee in November 1993 stated that United States was pursing a policy of "preventive diplomacy" in South Asia "that seeks to persuade India and Pakistan to forgo a ballistic missile arms race that combined with the regions nuclear weapons capability could destabilize an already fragile situation"[9].

In pursuit of the above objectives the United States has followed a step-by-step regional based approach, which complements its broader global efforts. As the US Assistant Secretary of State for Asia, Robin Raphel, said..... "our approach to halting proliferation and reducing tension in South Asia is fully consistent with our global approach to stopping proliferation"[10].

From the point of view of the theory of international relations there is no unanimity on why one nation gets interested in the affairs of another. Theoretical paradigms range from the out right cynical to being foolishly altruistic. The national interest paradigm, which is the off-cited explanation, is closer to cynical model than to the altuistic model[11].

A nation's vital interests are those for which it is prepared to engage in a military action, irrespective of the cost involved[12].

Preservation of such interests is accorded the highest priority that even military action is regarded as a legitimate act. Perhaps that is why aggression has often been justified by its perpetators as absolutely necessary for the security of the nation. However, it need be mentioned here that a superpower's perceptions of threat is not merely confined to an attack on home territories, but may include threats that are much more distant in space. Threats to the sources of important raw materials supply lines and allies, could constitute a threat that warrants a firm response from a superpower. The nature and the degree of response depends on the thinking of the incumbent administration. The agreed response is then translated into what is commonly referred to as strategic objectives, which infact are more specific goals calculated to serve those vital interests[13].

US interests and objectives in South Asia in 1990s retain traditional emphasis on American political / ideological goals, military security and commercial benefit, irrespective of disintegration of USSR, and the US remaining the only super power in the world, and notwithstanding the surfacing of societal concerns for environmental, gender and human rights issues, and some non-official Indo-US cooperation. The concept of "comprehensive security" and cooperation toward that goal have not yet, infused the American and South Asia policy-making circles. This is despite that fact that South Asian is home to approximately twenty percent of the world's people, and their success or failure in dealing with the myriad problems of uneven modernization facing them, will inevitably effect comfort levels in the entire world, including the US[14].

However, as officially articulated, US interests and objectives in South Asia are mainly: to prevent or halt the proliferation of weapons of mass destruction and missiles, to prevent the outbreak of war between India and Pakistan, to encourage economic reforms towards liberalization and privatization throughout the region, and expand trade, access to markets and direct financial investment, to promote democracy and respect for human rights, and to gain cooperation to curb illegal 'narcotics traffic as well as terrorism.

These US interests have marked the post-cold war global thrust of American foreign policy, to which South Asia is peripheral rather than central, and in which India and Pakistan are regarded as more important and more complicated than the other states[15].

American expectations generated by victory in the cold war as well as the immediately following Gulf War were epitomized in such phrases as President George Bush's, "New World Order" and Francis Fukuyama's, "the end of history". Such attitudes expressed in the construction of international regimes on technology or the reshaping of international economic institutions, for example, were distinctly ethnocentric and hegemonic[16].

They implicitly blurred distinctions between the US and the world, as a whole, attempted to harness the United Nations and other international institutions to US national purposes, presumed indefinite and unchallenged American dominance in cultural, economic, military and moral domains, and drew sustenance not only from actual US technological achievements and economic dynamism, but also from the superficially world wide appeal of American consumerism and popular entertainment. But assumption of 'unipolarity' combined with some particularities of US negotiating style in bilateral and multilateral forums, frequently left South Asian governments feeling that their legitimate concerns and interests had been overlooked as inconsequential by American counterparts[17].

These hurt feelings, which may well be more important than negotiable variances of national interests, were evident in India during the final stage of the Uruguay Round of GATT talks, the Singapore meeting of the World Trade Organization in December, 1996, and throughout the protracted debates on the indefinite extension of the Nuclear Non Proliferation (NPT) in 1995, and the opening of a Comprehensive Test Ban Treaty (CTBT) for signature in 1996, but are not absent elsewhere in the region. Hurt feelings frequently translate into some variant of anti-Americanism in public opinion, reluctance to deal freely with an issue of mutual concern, and governmental rejection of defiance of American hegemony that cannot be, therefore effortless, and must be maintained by exerting greater pressure to lesser effect[18].

This is particularly evident on nuclear issues, where the lack of US consideration for India's legitimate security concerns, and political need for definite commitment on the part of existing nuclear weapons power for the total elimination of nuclear weapons world wide, in a reasonable time frame, contributed greatly to New Delhi taking a much harder line of keeping its own options open in 1995-96 than in 1994, when India did not openly oppose indefinite extension of the NPT and jointly sponsored the CTBT resolution with the US.

The euphoric moment of victory in the cold war passed without stimulating internationally oriented idealism or compassion comparable to that earlier phase of US hegemony, immediately after the end of World War II. The American public showed a marked disinclination to expend its own blood and treasure on foreign intervention or uplift, and fears were expressed in some quarters of a new isolationism. Some saw a profound identity crisis in the US following the disintegration of Soviet Union and an absence of national strategy[19].

Perhaps to counter that tendency for more solid reasons of bureaucratic interests or arms production and sales, perhaps because of genuine feelings of insecurity in a rapidly changing world, it appeared as if some influential Americans were looking around for new enemies on the world stage[20]. Their apprehension were best expressed in Harvard University Singapore's Kishore Mahbubani phrase, 'The West and the Rest' which was soon converted into 'the West versus the Rest'.

"The Clash of Civilizations" written by Samuel P. Huntington, postulates violent conflict along the fault lines between civilizations both at the micro and macro levels most likely between the West and Islam and the West and China[22].

South Asia has been listed as 'Hindu' and one of seven major living civilizations the Indian Subcontinent has been referred to as an area for probable conflict with Islam. Some Hinduists tend to see the possibility of an anti-Islamic partnership with the US and Washington realizes a need to bolster Pakistan as a 'moderate' Islamic state restoring democracy and trims its policies in South Asia accordingly. Pakistan could be an asset for the US as it moves to replace economic dependence on Russia among the newly - independent republics of Central Asia and provide their exports of petroleum and other raw materials access to the sea, by passing both Russia and Iran. In the calculation of the US Central Command, Pakistan could also act as a southern military- naval anchor to the US dual containment of Iran and Iraq in the Persian Gulf. These strategic needs of the US probably underlay Washington's reasoning for 'normalizing' relations with Pakistan, and restoring some military and economic assistance through the flank Brown Amendment of 1995, that modified the Pressler Amendment of 1985 banning all assistance to Pakistan, if it continued with its nuclear weapons Programme.

United States is now turning its attention towards peace making role in the more complicated region. A general trend in post-cold war American policy of direct importance to South Asia is the adoption by the US of the role of mediator and peacemaker, promoter of human rights and democracy. South Asia is, of course, infinitely more important than other regions. It is the only region in the Third World where both (India and Pakistan) hostile neighbours are armed with nuclear weapons. And it lies in the vicinity of Persian Gulf, Iran, Central Asia, Russia and China, areas of vital interests of the US. Some events, which have altered US perceptions and policies and helped pave the way for a new US profile in South Asia, could be counted.

Pakistan's ruling elite is yet to recover from the rude shock it was dealt by the United States when it abruptly ditched its long-standing cold war ally, which was in fact instrumental in winning America's battle against the Soviet Union in Afghanistan. But like most ruling elite, dependent on external props, the Pakistani ruling establishment is a poor student of history.

As a result, in one of the bitter ironies of contemporary history, India, once the Soviet Union's best friend in the Third World, is today clearly the victor of the cold war in South Asia, whereas Pakistan, considered America's "most allied ally" during the cold war, is at the receiving end of pressures and policies emanating from the United States, which are clearly tilted towards India on such issues as Kashmir, due to fear of Islamic fundamentalism".

In January 1990, Pakistan's Chief of Army Staff General Aslam Beg, visited Iran and held cordial discussions with his Iranian counterparts. This sparked a debate and for the first time the US officially informed him that Pakistani support for the insurgency in "Occupied Kashmir" could be considered by the US as tantamount to "aiding and abetting terrorism". Interestingly, this marked the first time that the United States threatened to slap any country with a terrorism label over a conflict in which no American lives had been lost and no American nationals had been made the target of terrorism. President Bush sent his Deputy National Security Advisor, Robert Gates (director of CIA), to Pakistan and India for urgent discussions on Kashmir and nuclear issues. The Gates-Mission concluded without any meeting with Prime Minister Benazir Bhutto who was out of the country at that time.

Secondly, in September 1990, the US suddenly decided to invoke the Pressler Amendment by giving a new interpretation to the law, and stated that Pakistan was putting together components with which it could build a nuclear device. This law was invoked at a time when Pakistani troops had been sent to Saudi Arabia under American auspices following the Iraqi occupation of Kuwait

Finally, during the ensuing Gulf War, anti-American sentiments became widespread in Pakistan and most of the 5,000 American living in the country were promptly evacuated. Although Pakistan had troops stationed in Saudi Arabia while the war raged, Americans asked India and Sri Lanka to provide refuelling facilities for war planes headed towards the gulf. India promptly, obliged albeit in a covert manner[23].

This shows that recent US policy vis-a-vis South Asia, is two-pronged, it is directed to encourage India-Pakistan settlement on the Kashmir dispute and is also aimed at supporting an Islamabad New Delhi understanding on the nuclear issue. US-South Asian relations are also shaped by growing cooperation in economic and commercial fields.

One basic assumption about the US policy toward South Asia is that now relations have an economic agenda as well as military and security considerations. The issue is not reverting to the old style relations that existed during the cold war years, but to reorient these on economic and commercial grounds. Cooperation in the areas of anti-terrorism and controlling drug trafficking is a marked departure from the traditional mode of US-Pak relations, and the looming threat of hostilities breaking out it is not unrealistic to expect the United States to play a meaningful role in preventing this from happening. As for US mediation from resolving the India-Pakistan conflict over Kashmir and the nuclear issue, some circles expect to see the launch of peace process in South Asia.

Peace Prospects with special Reference to Kashmir

Nothing has bedevilled Indo-Pakistan relations more than the dispute over the beautiful mountainous state of Jammu and Kashmir. It is a fact of Indo-Pak relations that failure to resolve Kashmir dispute at bilateral level has resulted in outside intervention. Till now India and Pakistan have fought three major wars in 1947, 1965 and 1971 and recently a covert war in Kargil over Kargil, but its fate is yet to be resolved. Keeping this view in centrality, this study seeks to analyze the US perception of the Kashmir tangle and its implications for Indo-Pak relations to enhance the peace in subcontinent

Both India and Pakistan have advanced several arguments to strengthen their respective claims over Kashmir. These arguments are conflicting and contradictory. It is generally believed that this is not merely a territorial dispute and there is a strong ideological component to the motives of the two states. Burke has observed that the main reason of the Kashmir dispute was the "antithetical nature of Hindustan and Islam"[24]. Similarly Joseph Korbel has observed: 'Kashmir involves the struggle between the Medieval Islamic theocracy of Pakistan and the modern secular state of India[25]'.

The Kashmir issue has been one of the focal points of American involvement in the region, and it dates from the earliest stages of its reference to the Security Council.

Initially, the United States was hesitant to become involved in the Kashmir problem. Near East Office Director Loy Henderson-soon to become ambassador to India-urged acting Secretary of State Robert Lovett to stay out of the dispute. He argued the United States was already over committed globally and should avoid" making a choice between giving support to the interests of India or Pakistan", should not, through their involvement, provide the Soviets an opening to mix into the affairs of South Asia[26]. But later, as cold war intensified, the United States got deeply interested in the Kashmir dispute. And in cooperation with the UK, the United States moved important resolutions in the Security Council over Kashmir, which to a great extent, shaped the US perception of the dispute at later stages.

The US stance on Kashmir was more influenced by its cold war strategies than the merits of the dispute. The US found golden opportunity in Kashmir dispute and its reference to the UN to establish its strategic interest in the region. The role of United States in the Kashmir conflict was part of an overall American design in the Third World and in particular South Asia. Philips Talbot, US Assistant Secretary for Near Eastern and South Asian Affairs, himself admitted in his address to the United Nations Association of Wichita on October 23, 1964 that "Kashmir is only one aspect of course, of our larger interests in the subcontinent of South Aisa"[27]. United States took the position that India was legally within its rights in Kashmir and that any activities on the part of Pakistan or other parties were in violation of this legality[28].

By the mid 1950's when Pakistan proved more adaptable to American foreign policy than did India, the United States became increasingly sympathetic towards Pakistan's position vis-à-vis Kashmir. This was reflected in the growing insistence by the US in the United Nations that the Kashmir problem be resolved by plebiscite, a measure, which New Delhi considered inimical to its interests. American policy in the Kashmir disputes is widely interpreted as a reaction to India's refusal to align itself with the United States in the cold war. This was confirmed in 1954 when America entered into an arms aid agreement with Pakistan. When the Kashmir issue was brought before the Security Council the United States showed an active interest and involvement in this dispute. Through the United Nations intervention in the area, the Truman Administration made attempts to bring peace to South Asia that conformed to its overall post war goals. America considered that the Kashmir conflict would jeopardize its unwavering goal of commerce, peace and security.

On various other occasions, Washington asserted that UN resolution, which called for a plebiscite continued to be valid and binding on India. At the same time there was some minority opinion in the US, which supported the Indian argument that a plebiscite as means of resolving the Kashmir dispute had been out dated by the march of events in recent years. This opinion would agree with the statement to the Security Council by Gunnar Jarring in April 1957, that, "the implementation of international agreement of an adhoc character, which has not been achieved fairly speedily, may become progressively more difficult because the situation with which they were to cope has tended to change[29].

The end of cold war brought about perceptible change in the US stance on the Kashmir issue. Now the United States felt that it needed Pakistan no more to contain Soviet Communism, and thus there was no need to adopt a pro Pakistani stance on Kashmir. These post cold war changes in the US perception of the Kashmir dispute was first witnessed in 1990, at the peak of the crisis in Kashmir.

The Kashmir solution that the US may end up peddling is one that, in the ultimate analysis, strengthens the status quo and makes Kashmir an "autonomous region" under Indian occupation[30]. Thus in the early years of 1990s the United States had agreed to accept the validity of the "Simla Agreement" as the basis for the settlement of the Kashmir dispute between India and Pakistan. Accepting the validity of Simla Agreement it was also expected that US might re-launch the Dixon Plan for Kashmir. Named after its author, Sir Owen Dixon, who was the UN representative for India and Pakistan in 1950, the plan envisaged a division of Kashmir between India and Pakistan. Pt. Jawahar Lal Nehru had favoured the Dixon Plan, but it was a non-starter because Liaquat Ali Khan the Prime Minister of Pakistan rejected the proposal. The Dixon Plan proposed two ways for implementing a solution to the Kashmir dispute. The first option envisaged several plebiscites, area by area, in the whole of the disputed territory of Kashmir. Each designated area would then be allowed to India and Pakistan depending on the outcome of the voting. The alternative was to allocate parts of Kashmir with known preferences toward India or Pakistan to the respective countries without holding a plebiscite. A referendum would be limited only to those parts of Kashmir where both India and Pakistan claimed support in their favour[31].

The objective of these initiatives was to persuade Islamabad and New Delhi to seriously discuss the future of Kashmir.

On several occasions Kashmir has emerged as an important issue before the US Administration. In 1993, during John Mallot's (Principal Deputy Secretary of State for South Asian Affairs) visit to New Delhi an official statement was made on the Kashmir dispute. He stated that there are three basic motives, which govern the US position:

(i) We consider all of Kashmir to be disputed "territory, on both sides of the line of control.

(ii) This is an issue to be settled peacefully by India and Pakistan taking the wishes of the Kashmiris both Muslims and non – Muslims, into account; and,

(iii) The United States is prepared to be helpful in this process, if that is desired by both sides.

He suggested that "it is time for India and Pakistan to begin seriously to resolve the issue between them and put an end to 'their' cold war" [32].

The most dramatic aspect of Mallot's remark was the stress on taking the views of the Kashmiri people on both sides - a stand which has not been taken before.

Voice of America (VOA) reported that Ms. Robin Raphel, Assistant Secretary of State for South Asia, presented a five-point formula of Washington's policy regarding Indian occupied Kashmir. According to her, the US considered Kashmir a disputed territory and its future should be decided, keeping in view the wishes of the Kashmiris, through a dialogue between India and Pakistan.[33] The official US policy on Kashmir was stated in a press conference of regional press correspondents in March 1995 in Washington D.C. by Ms. Robin Raphel, she said,

> "...... our view on the status of Kashmir has not changed. We still are of the view that the geographical area of former princely state of Jammu and Kashmir and the entire geographic area is disputed territory. Our view remains the same. In terms of the US role, we are of the view that the dispute over Kashmir needs to be resolved by India and Pakistan, sitting down at the table seriously engaging in negotiations on that issue. We also believe that for any resolution to be stable and long-lasting, the wishes of the Kashmiri People have to take into account."

Referring to a question about US mediation to resolve the Kashmir dispute, she argued that:

> "..... if both India and Pakistan wished for a more explicit US role in solving the Kashmir dispute. We will be happy to do that. In Pakistan we have often heard, for example, why don't you mediate like you have done in West Asia. I have always replied to that in order to be a mediator you have to be accepted as such by both sides. In this case we do know Pakistan wishes it but India does not for its own

reasons. Therefore, we have not been able to play a role. But we stand and meanwhile we do what we can to encourage the two governments to sit down and talk about it"[34].

Although the United States has been interested in the Kashmir dispute from very beginning, the recent activism is due to several reasons. According to Tom A. Travis the American policy stance probably had three aims:

(i) Reference to the wishes of the Kashmiri people may have been intended to encourage India to be more attentive to the internal source of the Kashmir dilemma.

(ii) To exemplify the US role as the world's leading power and its concomitant responsibility to provide leadership to solve global conflict

(iii) To soften up India for concessions on issues like NPT, MTCR, GATT etc.[35]

The US Kashmir activism is also due to the fear of a nuclear war in the subcontinent over Kashmir, as this impression was created by Pakistan. The move to link Kashmir issue to non-proliferation and "nuclear terrorism" has been a theme that has been assiduously built up ever since the Clinton Administration took office. The US policy makers perceive that since both India and Pakistan posses the nuclear device and there is every possibility of the two going to war over Kashmir, as they have fought in 1947, 1965, 1971 and 1999. This situation does not help promote its economic interests. So American wants to brings both the countries into the NPT fold and chose Kashmir issue which is central to both India and Pakistan. To pressurize them to do so, Stephen Cohen has argued that "the road to accession to the NPT runs through Kashmir"[36]. The United States sees a close link between regional instability, the regional nuclear programme of India and Pakistan, and the Kashmir issue.

In short, the present US perceptions of Kashmir can be summed as follows:

(i) The US views the whole of Kashmir as disputed territory on both sides of the LoC, and that India and Pakistan should resolve the issue between them as agreed in Simla Agreement.

(ii) US might re-launch the Dixon Plan.

(iii) The United States no longer supports a plebiscite in Kashmir.

(iv) The US accepts Kashmiris as the third party in the issue.

(v) India needs to clean up its act in terms of human rights violations in the valley and try to restore some semblance of governance.

(vi) Kashmir will increasingly lead to heightened tensions between India and Pakistan, possibly resulting in another regional conflict, this time involving nuclear weapons.

(vii) The US believes that peace in the South Asian region would remain brittle as long as the Kashmir issue remains unsettled and unresolved.

(viii) The US offers its good offices to resolve the Kashmir dispute if parties to dispute agree so[37].

Despite history of mistrust, between the two countries however, there are reasons to be optimistic, that future conflicts can be avoided and that these states can work out for resolving their differences. Perhaps the most important reason for optimism in South Asia today is a sense of confidence on both sides that conflict resolution is the norm. Disagreements and misunderstandings are still common, but an underlying sense that India and Pakistan can work out their differences without resort to arms, seems to mark their interactions. As the only super power in the post cold war world, the US can play a very important and positive role in this region of turmoil, but it will have to tread very carefully to proceed in establishing peace in the South Asian region.

Reference:

1. Paranjpe Shrikant, 'US Nonproliferation Policy in Action: South Asia, Sterling New Delhi 1987, No.19, p. 46.
2. Lavoy R. Peter: "Learning and the Evolution of Cooperation in US and Soviet Non Proliferation Activities" in Breslauer W. George and Tetlock E. Philip, (eds.) Learning in US and Soviet Foreign Policy (Boulder Colarode West view, 1991).
3. See April 28, 1993 Congressional testimony of John R. Mallott, Deputy Assistant Secretary of State for South Asian Affairs.
4. Galbraith Peter, "Nuclear Proliferation in South Asia: "Whose Business" in Raghvan Sulochana et. el. Conflicting. Image: India and the United States, Reverdale Maryland, 1990, p.70.
5. Editorial The Times of India (New Delhi) April 11,1994 p.1.
6. Indian Express (Chandigarh) March 26,1994, P. 1.
7. Cohen P. Stephen, "Nuclear Neighhours" in S.P. Cohen, ed. No. 3. pp. 2-3.
8. Joshi Manoj: "Separate US deals for India, Pak on N-Issue". The Times of India (New Delhi) 9 April 1994, P-1.
9. The Statesman, New Delhi, November 93, P.27.
10. Raphel Robin, "America and South Asia" Span Vol. XXXIV, No. 11, November 93, P.27.
11. Rao, Chandrashekhar R.V.R "The US and the Indian Subcontinent: Can there be a Regional Detente" in Cruden M. Robert, Joshi Manoj, Rao Claandrashekhar R.V.R. (eds.) No.1, pp. 111-112.
12. Brodie Burnard "Vital Interests: By Whom and How Determined in Trager F.N. and Krosenberg P.S. (eds.) National Security and American Society, University Press of Kansas, Lawerence 1973, pp. 63-67.
13. Cronin Richard, "United States Interests Objectives and Policy Options in South West Asia" in Kheli Tahir Shirin (ed) US Strategic Interest in South West Asia, Prager, New York, 1982.
14. The Asian Society Study Mission cited earlier explicity recognized that the most compelling security challenges facing India and its neighbours stem from social and economic issues. It recommended US government and private financial and technical support to regional South Asian bodies tackling such issues, including environmental protection, harnessing water resources and improving transport and communications. Study Mission, n. 4, p. 43.

15. Thornton Perry Thomas, "US Relations with India and its Neighbours" in Hussain A Noor and Rose E Leo (eds.) Pakistan - US Relations: Social Political, Economic Factors Berkely' Institute of East Asian Studies University of California, 1998, P. 160-82.
16. Hegemony is understood as means to effortless and recognized superiority in all fields of human activity, material and moral, and ethnacentrism to mean an embodying higher values and moves than others.
17. For an illuminating study of the negotiating style of the US, which underestimates the importance of effective ties and obligations of status especially in dealing with Egypt, India, Japan and Mexico, see Cohen Richered, Negotiating Across Culture Washington, DC. US Institute for Peace Studies 1995.
18. Thornton Perry Thomas (eds.), Anti Americanism: Origin and Context, The American Academy of Political and Social Science, The Annals May 1933.
19. America's greatness as a superpower was to a large extent, a function of the threats that it overcome, particularly Soviet nuclear and conventional military risks. With the disappearance of the primary threat, US power is diminished in both relative and absolute terms: Keel E. Carl, "Toward a New National Strategy: The Need for Immediacy" in Sommerville (ed.) Essay on Strategy', Washington, D.C.: National Defence University Press 1993 pp. 45-74.
20. Special Report on the Weapons Bazar in the US in the US New and World Report, 9 December 1996.
21. Huntington P. Samuel, "The Clash of Civilizations"? Foreign Policy Summer 1993, P. 22-49.
22. The Herald August 1996, pp. 39-40.
23. Burke, S.M., "Pakistan's Foreign" Oxford University Press, Oxford 1973, pp. 10-11.
24. Korbel Joseph No.1.
25. Kux Dennis, Estranged Democracies: India and the United States 1941-91, Sage Publications, New Delhi 1993, P.60.
26. Department of State Bulletin, Vol. II, No. 1325, November 16, 1964, P. 702.
27. The American representatives in United Nations endorsed the Indian Position: "External sovereignty of Jammu and Kashmir to India this foreign sovereignty went over to India and is excercized

by India and that is how India happens to be here as a petitioner" quoted in Patwant Singh, India and the Future of Asia, Knoff A Alfred, New York, 1966, p. 152.

28. UN Security Council, Report on the India - Pakistan Question Submitted in Pursuance of the Resolution of the Security Council of 21 February 1957, 5/3393, 3/3821, April 29, 1957, p. 6.
29. The Herald August 1996, p. 40.
30. Nayar KP, "US Reviving Dixon Plan in Bid to End Kashmir Row", Indian Express (New Delhi) 19 December 1994.
31. For the text of John Mallote's speech at India International Centre, New Delhi May 1993, see, Strategic Digest July 1993, pp. 57-60.
32. The Nation (Lahore) 26 March 1994.
33. Kashmir: USA Offers to Mediate" The Tribune (Chandigarh) 3 March 1995.
34. Travis A. Tom, "Indo-American Relations: The Kashmir Controversy" India Quarterly Vol. XLIX, No. 4, Oct. - Dec. 1993, p. 54.
35. The Indian Express (New Delhi) March 2, 1994.
36. Alam Aftab, "US Policy Towards South Asia", Raj Publications, 1998.

5

Impact of 9/11: Changing Phenomena of Security and Indo-Pak Relations

History, in its hitherto documented form of civilizational progress, bears testimony to the fact that the 20th century civilization has been the bloodiest and violent of all. The tragedy of the 20th century is that it began with the promise of bringing an end to war as an investment of state diplomacy, but is ending as the world's bloodiest century, with 108 million war dead[1]. No doubt that man in modern civilization has come to find himself to be more the victim of his civilization than being its creator and master. Despite the fact that even the modernized western nations face several problems generated by the socio economic and political advocacies of modern civilization, it is the real pinch of these adversities. Not only are they characterized by numerous inherent weaknesses of their system but also are still reeling under the pressures of imperialistic forces.

In the nuclear age, and now the age of bio-terrorism, and in the wake of September 11th, 2001, it is also imperative that we find ways to resolve our conflict, short of violence[2]. It is also a turning point in world history to define the concept of security. Its many facets and the likely mechanism to control this because on that date one world ended another was born. As a result of this event, policy decision and future choices may well be driven by a blurring of concerns that involve state centric security. The implications for the analysts and policy makers are tremendous. We may be witnessing a "boomerang effect" in which we must focus both on aspects of national and human security and must

Alternative 'Security' Concept

Tradition and origin	Forms of Security	Specific Emphasis		
		Focus Security	What is at risk	Threats to
Traditional, realist based	National Security	The State	- Sovereignty - Territorial integrity	Other States (and non-state actors in post-Cold War)
Both traditional and non-traditional, realist-and liberal based	"Social" Security	- Nations - Societal groups - Class and economic focus - Political action committees / interest groups	- National unity - Quality of life - Wealth distribution	- States themselves - Nations - Migrants - Alien culture
Non-traditional - liberal base	Human Security	- Individuals - Mankind - Human right - Rule of Law	- Survival - Human development - Human development	- The State itself Globalization Natural catastrophe and change

Contd...

Tradition and origin	Forms of Security	Specific Emphasis		
		Focus Security	What is at risk	Threats to
Non-traditional, potentially extreme	Environmental Security	The Ecosystem	Global sustainability	Mankind through resource depletion, scarcity, war and ecological destruction

realize that excessive focus on one aspect of security at the expense or detriment of the other may well cause us to be "boomeranged" by a poor balancing of ends and means in a changing security environment

Terrorism has a singular goal to cause terror! Tear! Terrorism undermines faith in the establishment. It weakens the enemy from within... causes interest in the masses. In this way, terrorism becomes a political weapon and removes a government's facade of infallibility, thus shocking its people's faith... this is exactly what happened in the USA on 9/11. This single terrorist attack on world's super power unimagined, unexpected and uncalled for, changed the security perceptions all over the world immediately. The USA which was sermonizing India to deal with terrorism peacefully and was unable to grasp India's concerns overnight became acutely sensitive to terrorism and its ramifications. This single terrorist - success made nation's see threats such activities posed to sovereign nation's whose primary duty is to protect and safeguard their citizen's life for which the state exists - the very raisond etre of states being. As a result human security in all its dimensions has become important in all discussions of security. Since 9/11 the need to establish peace though CBMS to enhance national as well as human security has become paramount in all discussions at the highest level of governance in both the developing and the developed worlds.

The implications of the changing security landscape for the analysts and policy makers are therefore potentially tremendous. In essence, we must focus on both aspects of "national security", in which military forces may continue to play a preeminent role, as well as human security in which "non traditional" security issues dominant. Thus, we may well witness renewed focus on failed or failing states, environmental stress, resource scarcity and depletion, drugs, terrorism, small arms, inhuman weapons, cyberwars and narco-traffiking. As desperate as these non-traditional security aspects indeed are, they all will have great influence on future strategic relationships and decisions. The issue truly is not one of "hard" traditional security, or "soft" non-traditional security. The future will require decision makers in both the developing and developed world to focus on a broad understanding of the meaning security.

Traditionally, when we use the term "security" as we assume these three basic questions, they are: Security from what? Security by whom? Security achieved through which means? In making assumptions about security, various "grand strategies" seek to focus on what levels of security matter, which are less relevant, and what means and mechanisms are best suited to fulfil the basic need to be "secure". Various concepts of security that are most prevalent today are in a simple format:

In the overall scheme of security alternatives above, what may well be changing is the notion that of all the issues of security, issues of national security matter most. Security, whether one insists on a distinction between hard and soft security, is about more than protecting the country from external threats. Security may well include critical infrastructure protection, economic security, social security, environmental security and human security.

The idea of security as a basic concept is frequently applied in international relations and in analysis of policy decisions, its essential meaning is often more widely diagnosed than agreed on[4].

As one result, we frequently see the proliferation of descriptions added to the basic concept itself. Each of these descriptions lends a perhaps slightly different connotation as well. When we speak of economic, geographic gender, cultural, environmental, ethnic, military, physical, psychological, political, social or human security, do we speak of a common identity or do we simply fragment security identities into separate categories, each clearly distinct from the other? This broadening understanding of security, of course, is part of the problem. In essence "security" becomes so wide an understanding that its relevance takes on all things to all people

- or nothing to no one, as the case may be. As Emma Rothschild argued in a essay titled –"What Is Security? The Quest for World Order" the principles and definitions of security, through well established in international politics have traditionally been of greatest importance to the "ceremonials of reconstructions" after large international wars.

History, in the Indian sub-continent, is an album of surprises. The tussle between India and Pakistan is more than half century old. It has witnessed four open bitter wars, a long proxy war and unending grappling. It has cost many crore rupees and of lakhs of lives. Because the bloodshed, the expenditure has been chronic, but there has been attrition and the damage to both the counties has been enormous. Both urgently need harmony peace and end to deadly conflicts. This is because Dr. Mehbub-Ul-Haq a renowned Pakistani scholar and special advisor to the United Nations Development Programme Administration, while releasing the Human Development Report 1992 said–

If Pakistan and India freeze their military expenditure at its current level during the years 1990s they could reap peace dividend of 50 million dollars during the current decade enough to put all their children in schools, provide preliminary health call, and clean drinking water to everyone, and to banish malnutrition by 2000. Even solution to basic problems of the people of India sub-continent lie in their unity, understanding co-operation and mutual trust[5]. The reality for the India and Pakistan, is that there is a foreground focus on two main issues–the war on terrorism and homeland security. However, conflicts arise because sometimes we attach too much importance to secondary matters such as differences in political or economic systems including rat race. There seems to be much discrimination caused by these differences. But happily, comparatively basic human well-being is not based on these things. All these different philosophies or religious systems are supposed to serve human happiness. But there is some thing wrong when there is too much emphasis on these secondary matters.

It is important to keep in mind that any peace-building process and its implementation in the Third World countries to be meaningful has to address itself not only to the general problem of peace faced by the world but also to the specific problems of peace faced by these third world countries. The problem faced by third world countries range from the politico-economic field to socio-cultural and ecological one[6]. In the third world countries dialogues are not the only condition to face problems, they are none the less essential ingredients because we are living in the age of transparency. Not that we are more straight forward and honest than before, but because we are constantly being watched and spied. The media is faster mode of communications, spy planes and satellites, electronic eavesdropping are furiously encroaching upon our privacy, more so the public life of our leaders and of our civil servants, and more vital activities of our armed forces. It is thus easy to destroy the economy of a country by shattering its investment by pushing goods into its market, or getting associated with its enterprises.

The problem to make a peaceful world is not an abstract but of concrete and immediate necessity and of highest priority. It is not nuclear, but technological advancement that has threatened world safety. The 9/11 is a current examples of that. Before us, we have two alternatives. Either to continue the process of hatred, or to decide resolutely to start intensive and constructive efforts to eliminate war, violence, the use of force and to prepare securities for life in peace. For pursuing the second alternative, some beginning has to be made. Let us not touch the disputed issues. Bilateral trade, cultural and educational exchange should get precedence over disputed matters. Importance of education and leadership in these areas along with other areas necessary for a more peaceful world and to commit time resources to ensure that this occurs. Let there be heart to heart talk between the people of both countries. Visa and other travelling facilities should be provided easily. This can create a lot of goodwill. Mistrust can be replaced by trust and once it is done, the problems of Kashmir and Karachi will evaporate. It is unification time and not division, and no more divisions. Unification is the call of the time. A divided world argues badly for the human family in the 21st century. Bernard Lown, reminded India of her role to be played for the betterment of the World and said.

"India, blessed with an ancient legacy of rich, cultural pluralism and a unique religious and spiritual imagination can play a key role in shaping a human world order for the 21st century and beyond. Of great urgency is to assist in re-balancing lives and moral imperatives, enable human beings to cope with the global crisis of the spirit to assume that role demands a manifest political resolve for tolerance of communal diversity and the cultivation of the free play of pluralistic dialogue among India's diverse multitudes"[6]. In Yajurveda, we see prayer for a peaceful world.

Om! May there be peace in the sky and in space!

May there be peace on land and in the waters!

May herbs and food bring us peace.

May all the personifications of God bring us peace.

May God bring us peace.

May there be peace throughout the world!

May the peace be peaceful. May God give me such peace!

Om! May there be peace (physical peace), peace (mental peace) and peace (spiritual peace) Om!

(Yajurveda Ch. 36 Hy. 17)[8]

The same vision we can find in Islam because Muslim ethics is one of the greatest virtues that Islam teaches. It also punches the scethics of brotherhood of men and service of humanity[9]. A dream is seen by Muhammad Iqbal; Models of unifications, integration are before us because world is shrinking. Globalisation is the creed now. In the recent years we have seen the union of Vietnam, the collapse of Berlin Wall, and the disappearance of communism. The sworn enemies of yesterday have become bosom friends, rather brothers. Germany can unite, Vietnams can unite. Efforts are being made to unite South and North Korea. The same can happen here also. "Vasudhaiva Kutumbakam" is an old adage here, and is a part of India's global vision. However, the search for peace must continue. Because the ultimate logical conclusion of war is amihilation. We wish to improve relations with our neighbours. We know that the easiest way to win a war is not to let it happen. We are to hold talks with Pakistan on any subject, at any level and at any time[10].

References

1. Ruth Legar Siward, World Military and Social Expenditures World Priorities Inc. Washington D.C. 1966, p. 7.
2. Linda Groff, Intercultural and Inter religious Dialogue: Towards a More Peaceful World. ed. Naresh Dadhich. Aalekh Publication, p.30.
3. P.H. Liotta, Impact of 9/11: Convergence of National and Human Security, Towards a More Peaceful World. ed. Naresh Dadhich. Aalekh Publication, p.70.
4. Ibid, p.71.
5. M.G. Chitkara, Indo Pak Relations Challenges before New Millennium. APH Publishing Corporation, p. XVL.
6. Arie Nadler, Reconciliation Between Enemy Nations: A Socio-Psychological Analysis Towards a More Peaceful World, ed. Naresh Dadhich. Aalekh Publication, p.121.
7. Bernard Lawn, "New World Order and Globalism", The Tribune December 23, 1993, p. 8.
8. One of the oldest composed text in human history approx. 1500 B.C.
9. Dr. Kedar Nath Tiwari, Comparative Religion. Motilal Banarasi Das (1983, Reprint, 1987), p.168.
10. Atal Behari Vajpayee, address to the Nation from Red Fort, New Delhi, August 15, 1998.

6

Epilogue

On the basis of discussion in the preceding chapters, one can now attempt to present an over all view of the South Asian spectrum with special reference to Indo-Pakistan relations and peace prospects. End of the cold war, collapse of USSR and all-system and drastic changes in nuclear policies of both India and Pakistan help us to draw broad conclusions about the future prospects of peace in the South Asian region.

Though Indo-Pak relations are bilateral in nature, their mutual relations and course of actions have been influenced by the actions and pronouncements of extra regional actors. The US has been the most important state, which has had profound influence on the policy and perceptions of these two neighbours.

The initial American involvement in Asia was primarily the product of its global policy of the containment of communism. The emergence of communist China in 1949, coupled with professed Soviet intervention of internationalizing communism, led many Americans to believe that without Western assistance Asian nationalism might not be an impediment to expanding communism. In congruence with its containment policy, the Americans sponsored a system of security alliance on the periphery of the communist world. They were willing to sign up for their team all those players who exhibited some interests in checking the onward march of communism. They did not bother to analyze closely the factors and compulsions of these regional players. The US-South Asian policy has also been framed in accordance with these objectives. The US is not an Asian power. Its attention is only focused on the region in times of crisis in the area, be it regional conflict or a heightened perception of the Soviet threat. Thus the relevance of the region has witnessed fluctuations with evolving American relation with the Soviet Union and China.

A sense of insecurity and helplessness during Pakistan's early years pushed that country into the arms of the Americans. Without giving much thought to its immediate geopolitical realities Pakistan joined SEATO and CENTO in order to balance the perceived Indian threat and to acquire much needed economic and military assistance. The Americans accepted Pakistan's participation in their collective security arrangement, without properly comprehending the nature and intensity of the deep rooted Indo-Pakistan hostility.

Although both Pakistan and the United States entered the alliance with a view to serve their own national interests, neither fully understood the implications and consequences of an alliance between unequal partners. The Americans never contemplated the use of US supplied equipment, or US forces against India. The Pakistanis on the other hand, expected that the Americans would not only extend full diplomatic support to Pakistan's case on Kashmir but would also actively back Pakistan in the event of a war with India.

Although a little on the high side, Pakistani expectations were somewhat natural, because Pakistani thought that the Americans were not only fully conscious of the Indian threat to Pakistan's security, but also realized that this had been the main factor in Pakistan's decision to join the Western camp. Pakistan may have been naive in this, but its naivety was probably due to a lack of experience in diplomacy. Perhaps the Americans were just as naive, their experience as world policeman was limited. They were not able to judge the implications of an alliance between a superpower and a small power that was deeply enmeshed in a local conflict.

Pakistan benefited from its association with the United States in many ways. The association not only yielded much desired economic and military assistance but also infused confidence and psychological security against the perceived Indian threat. Similarly, the Americans gained from their association with Pakistan. Not only did they enlist Pakistan's support in establishing both the northern and southern tiers of their defence alliance system, they were able to maintain continuity in it, Pakistan being physically located at a point where the alliance system converged geographically. In addition, US received certain specific privileges from Pakistan, such as facilities for launching high attitude reconnaissance aircraft over Soviet or Chinese territories -significant privileges in the era before spy satellites. The Indian reaction to the US -Pakistan military relationship was strong and angry. Nehru accused America of introducing the cold war to the region. Irritated at the Eisenhower-Dulles policy, India moved closer to the Soviets hoping to balance the American presence. Despite the American interpretation of nonalignment as "immoral", the incumbent US administration thought fit to keep India assured of American friendship and readiness to provide military assistance.

Obviously the major American objective in this was to slow down or stop the Indian drift toward the Soviets. Thus economic aid continued to pour into India on much bigger scale than that allocated to Pakistan. This aid enabled India to allocate its own resources toward military requirements, and to pursue successfully its policy of nonalignment earning would wide prestige as a truly independent country whereas Pakistan was dubbed a subservient state.

America's soft policy toward India did not check the Chinese, neither did it balance Soviet influence in India, nor did it convince India of America's sincere wish to work for peace in the area. New Delhi regarded the US security relationship with Pakistan as destabilizing. Although Indian and US views converged on Suez, the Indian attitude over the Hungarian crisis lacked the bite reflected in its Suez policy. America chose to ignore the duality in Indian policy, and economic cooperation continued to grow.

The advent of the Kennedy administration registered a major change in Americans Indian policy. Not only did the new administration access non-alignment as an operative principle of international relations it admired democratic India. Because of the efforts of India's friends in the Kennedy administration, a much better understanding developed rather quickly. Apart from the administration's tilt toward India, other international development and advancement in technology, further paved the way for a closer association of the two countries. With the advent of reconnaissance satellites and ICBMs the Sino-Soviet rift, and the Sino-Indian border war, the Americans began to see as a counterpoise to China.

American regional policy moves from one end of the spectrum to the other in congruence with global and regional developments, rather than being based on a well calculated long term regional policy. American policy makers have rarely been able to understand the conflictual cobweb of South Asia, particularly in the past. Ultimately, the American contribution toward peace and stability of South Asia has not been as great as it should have been.

United States must apply a well throught out policy to an area and then develop calculated moves aimed at attaining US objectives events and sudden developments. Admittedly reactive moves may at times be necessary, but the US should not lose sight of long term regional objectives. Given the prevailing winds in South Asia, America can undertake many positive measures to enhance not only its security but also peace of South Asia. It should formulate its long-term objectives in South Asia, maintaining a certain amount of consistency. It should support as it has been, the ongoing process of Indo-Pakistan normalization and regional cooperation. This detente is the key to the emergence of a regional framework. It could eventually result in the establishment of an effective regional association, and a significant reduction in tension. One way to approach this objective is to channel all future aid through a collective regional framework. With a number of issues still in dispute and not under control, it is certainly appropriate to consider how security perceptions and mutual confidence can be reinforced.

Today, new arguments are emerging in New Delhi, Islamabad and Washington for "nuclear realism". Conceding that nuclear disarmament is beyond reach, both globally and in South Asia, and convinced that current diplomatic approaches have become counter productive, the new nuclear realists have set their sights on arms control and CBMs to avoid a nuclear war in the region. There are frequent appeals to recast India's nuclear policy from its present emphasis on global and normative consideration to a new focus on national security requirements. Strategic analyst Subrahmanyam and Sunderji accept the permanence of military capabilities in the region, and stress the need for India and Pakistan to learn to live peacefully in such an environment

CBMs the only way out

In the early 90s, New Delhi had embraced the concept of confidence building with Pakistan. Several concrete measures were negotiated and implemented by the two sides, and a high - ranking advisory group stressed the importance of confidence building and risk - reduction measures to prevent conflict with Pakistan.

Pakistan, too, had given isolated indications, of a willingness to move beyond the traditional posture of regional denuclearization in order to stabilize the region's nuclear reality. There are two problems which can escalate into a war—

(i) Kashmir Problem, and

(ii) Nuclear Weapons.

Both these spheres need extensive CBMs as early as possible.

Problem of Kashmir and Proposed CBMs

Kashmir is unique among all the crisis points in the Indo-Pak - US tangle. It is virtually inevitable before any effort for a peaceful solution can succeed.

If there were not the crisis of Kashmir, the question of parity and status with India would not have created as many hurdles in bilateral relations of two countries. It can be said that the Kashmir problem has increased the importance of Pakistan, seeking status and parity with India. Unless Pakistan surpasses India in military strength and capability, it cannot reverse the status quo in Kashmir. Pakistan has declared many times that if Kashmir problem is not solved than there will be a nuclear war between India and Pakistan.

The Punjab Provincial Assembly Speaker Mohammad Hanif Ramay, during Common wealth Seminar at Delhi had said, "We have been talking and talking. But, if we go on talking without meaning, we will have another war[1]. Armed conflicts reflecting the passions of man create a vicious circle. The lesson of history is that, instead of settling any problem finally, war creates more problems and generates greater tensions and results in another war, so have nuclear wars. It creates a chain reaction and an unending process continues. Late in life, Dr. Albert Einstein, was asked what weapons may be used in World War III. He said, "I do not know. But, I assure you that World War IV will be fought with stones[2]".

The analysis of the causes of war will show and establish without an iota of doubt, that wars settle nothing at all. Major wars since, 1947, may convince any prudent man of average ability that wars rather create and not solve the problems - notably Kashmir. Rather, it created economic problems in the Indian sub continent. The next war if it is waged, will be nuclear war, which will mean global destruction. There is no going away from talks, however long and exasperating. The solution has to be found patiently. It is patience and perseverance, which is likely to overcome even mountains, emphasized Mahatma Gandhi. The two countries should never snap dialogue.

It is time for both India and Pakistan to realise that by keeping their talk going, neither side is going, to do a favour to the other. As the relation, between the two areas are so bad, there is an overwhelming reason to keep talking rather than start fighting.

Both India and Pakistan should focus on employing practical ways and pragmatic approach, to resolve specific problems such as demilitarizing the Siachen Glacier, since India and Pakistan are both potential nuclear powers, it is all the more important that they settle their differences through negotiations. Dialogue must continue. A responsible approach to the Kashmir question must be in line with the longer term and larger vision of the subcontinent as a whole. In India and more so in Pakistan, there is a strongly held view that Kashmir must be, 'settled' first, and only then can India-Pakistan normalization follow or be facilitated.

A change to the status quo will only stand a chance of succeeding if in the process, it can dispel the long standing hostility and suspicion which has existed between India and Pakistan ever since 1947, and which perhaps explains why no lasting solution has ever been reached. Both countries in self-interest must strive to rediscover that the lesser evil is to work towards a climate of bilateral relations which afford scope for the plurality of religions and autonomy in Kashmir. Indian controlled and Pakistan occupied Kashmir could not be quarantined, from contacts across the ceasefire line indefinitely. To ensure a cooperative approach, Pakistan cannot forever be excluded from a non-political role and links with Kashmir. But to include Pakistan in a constructive involvement, the pre conditions is the chemistry of mutual trust. It must begin by not shirking from acknowledging that India and Pakistan cannot prosper in suspicion and hostility. India has to demonstrate, by deeds and not only by declarations, that it has sympathy and, where feasible, a stake in assisting Pakistan's own economic problems. India has to stoop, not to conquer, but to catalyze cooperation. But Pakistan too must by now, become more confident of its identity, independent of the Indian bogey, Pakistan's Foreign Policy must not revolve around the fear of India or a political crusade against it.

To facilitate this, it would be in common interest that the Kashmir problem should slide off the headlines and again recede into the limbo of officially unresolved problems. Amicable relations, cooperation, mutual understanding between the two, is not only must for permanent peace in the subcontinent, but also for correcting the past mistakes.

It is time to recollect the history of partition, as history teaches everything including the future. Partition, in the form that it finally took in the subcontinent, was a solution which the British brought themselves to accept with some reluctance. Many Britishers still bemoan the tragedy, which brought about the destruction of the united subcontinent, the master stroke of the British imperial genius.

As of today, the Indo-Pak relations are not so cordial. Divided we fall and united we stand. Both should realize the ground realities. Pakistan has said many times that if Kashmir problem is not solved then there will be a nuclear war between India and Pakistan. Many observers in 1947 hoped and believed that once the first difficult days of independence were over, India and Pakistan would settle down together in some kind of joint harness, combining their resources and their talents to solve vast social and economic problems facing the sub continent.

It may be remembered that sizeable military expenditures weaken any country in confronting domestic as well as global problems. India and Pakistan are no exceptions. If they both freeze their military expenditure at its current level during the 1990s, they could reap peace dividend of 50 billion dollars during the current decade– enough to put all their children in schools, provide primary health care and clear drinking water to everyone, and to banish malnutrition by 2001. Solution to the basic problem of the people of Indian sub - continent lie in their unity, understanding, cooperation, and mutual trust. Unfortunately, India and Pakistan are among the biggest arms importers in the world.

It is time that both, realized that by keeping their talks going, neither side is going to show a favour to the other. As the relations between the two areas are bad, there is an overwhelming reason to Keep an talking rather than start fighting. Both should focus on employing practical ways and pragmatic approach to resolve specific problems, such as demilitarising the Siachen Glacier. Since India and Pakistan are both potential nuclear powers, it is all the more important that they settle their differences through negotiations. There must be transparency in the steps, which would be taken by India and Pakistan.

At the outset, both had a great deal in common and shared many of the same cultural traditions and languages. Their leaders had been members of the same government service. They had been allies in the political struggle against the same opponent, the British. Indians and Pakistanis very well knew and understood each other. It is time to sit together and to rectify old mistakes. Let them sit together now. It is not too late to adopt the righteous path.

On the eve of the 21st century, Kashmir does not have luxury of a long period of introverted consolidations nor the resources to develop into an Asian Switzerland. The unity in Indian sub continent may emerge in a common market and a consideration of which a united Kashmir would, of course would be a proud member. Undeniably the resolve to solve Kashmir problem transparently, seeking solution outside the framework of the Indian constitution will automatically invite the wrath of all sections of the people, against the establishment, and trigger a chain reaction in other states and ethnic revivalism leading to further balkanization of Indian sub-continent.

Answer to Kashmir problem, undoubtedly, lies in the economic prosperity of the sub continent. The people should work in unison. People living in the sub continent are one, irrespective of their castes, religions, colour, creed and the regions. The remedy to the Kashmir imbroglio ultimately lies in unification of India and Pakistan. India need to chart out a clear-cut course of action to restore normalacy and stability in the valley.

Many face saving formulas both for India and Pakistan are being tossed about regarding the solution of the Kashmir problem. These are: —

1. The Indian government and Pakistan government should give the genuine autonomy to Kashmir in areas under their respective control.
2. There should be free movement of men and material across the Line of Control (LoC), both India and Pakistan armies should withdraw from the area while retaining minimum numbers for maintaining law and order. The situation should continue for at least five years, then the next step could be contemplated.
3. Both in India and Pakistan, not to speak of Kashmir, the majority of the people would prefer dialogue and reconciliation, though a vocal and aggressive minority would oppose such a policy. Therefore, "it is time for the so called 'silent majority' to express and assert its view of sanity; the governments of both the countries may be able to adopt their policies along the unbeaten track".
4. Restoration of the prestige and authority of the state administration which requires rooting out of corruption and cleansing in particular of the local police of disloyal and unscrupulous elements.
5. Return and rehabilitation of the 300,000 Kashmir Pandits and a lakh or so of the valley's Muslims émigrés in their homes is a task of top priority, which must be completed before preparations are made for elections in the State.
6. In the face of Pakistan's continuing violations of the line of control, our military should be authorized to counter-attack and straighten out the LOC, whereever it traverses in hospitable terrain at present.

7. The line should be fortified with an adequate number of semi-permanent and permanent military camps and cantonments along its entire length.
8. For all the money given to the State by the Union Government since 1947, the valley has little to show by way of economic development. Comprehensive regional plans for development of Kashmir and Jammu should be prepared. The highest priority should go to the creation of massive employment opportunities for the States youth within and in the rest of India.
9. The State's educational system is in need of attention, modernization and vocational orientation.
10. A new Department of Kashmir Affairs should be created in the Union Home Ministry to oversee the State's development activity and other affairs. It should have an eminent figure from the state at its head as Minister of State.
11. Advantage must be taken of the growing revulsion against militancy, but without talking of a political solution or initiating negotiations with militants.
12. To seal the borders, enough flexibility must be given to the security forces to deal with the situation, and attend to the needs of the people.

However, if a solution could be reached which involves a genuine dialogue on all sides appropriate to the world as it is in the 1990 and not how it was in 1947, India could take pride in having fulfilled its pledge to ascertain the will of the Kashmir people in determining their future. Pakistan would be free, at last from a national preoccupation and able to focus attention on developing valuable relations not only with India, but with the new Muslim republics in Central Asia.

If India and Pakistan go to war again over Kashmir, the world will express some sympathy, but is unlikely to energetically rescue the countries from chaos; if they disintegrate it will be a humiliation for our many cherished faiths and the mockery of the ancient civilization which inspires both countries. The need is to bring people of different faiths closer in order to strengthen humanity, and without a general acceptance on settlement the Kashmir issue is likely to remain indefinitely on the international agenda of unresolved conflicts, which may yet become more explosive. It is a testimony to the Kashmiris own endurance that despite all they have suffered, they are still looking forward to the day when their land will become "not a cot of hatred between India and Pakistan" but a bridge of friendship.

Nuclear Weapons and Proposed CBMs

An understanding is also emerging in United States that complete nuclear disarmament in South Asia may no longer be a feasible policy objective. Even after conducting the nuclear tests in 98, US continues to advocate Indian and Pakistani adherence to, NPT and its focus is on trying to achieve more immediate goals including the adoption of regional confidence building measures "such as ending all firing across the line of control and notifying each other of troop movements".

The strategic, political, bureaucratic and nationalistic forces at work in South Asia make it extremely unlikely that India and Pakistan will agree to roll back or cap their nuclear programme. These programmes are too advanced to be disbanded. Outside pressure is unlikely to change this situation. The only solution that can be implemented is the lowering of the nuclear weaponry to the level of "minimum deterrence" or "defensive defence". Thus, instead of pursuing the unattainable goal of seeking to induce India and Pakistan to give up their nuclear options, the United States should shift from a focus on non-proliferation in South Asia to a policy designed to maintain nuclear restraint. Such a policy would seek to freeze the stockpile of fissile material, the development of military related nuclear capabilities, and the development, production and deployment of nuclear weapons by both India and Pakistan.

As a result of the widespread interest in crisis management between India and Pakistan, a general theory of CBMs has emerged of late. The key question is how to stabilize deterrence during crisis while reducing the prospects of accidental or inadvertent war. This involves reducing the prospects of preemption, loss of control and unwanted escalation, each of which could have lead to a nuclear war that neither side wants. The management of the deterrent relationship between India and Pakistan, in particular nuclear crisis management, has become not only an important part of strategic thought in South Asia, but a policy preoccupation as well.

The two sides will have to embark on a course of re-instituting a whole range of confidence and security building measures to stabilize nuclear deterrence and prevent the drift toward an unwanted nuclear exchange during a crisis. These measures can be described as means to enhance, the stability in the region.

Extending the No-Attack Agreement:

1. No Attack Agreement: Indians and Pakistanis sometimes point out that their past wars have been relatively restrained. Loss of civilian life has been minimal, combat has been restricted to the battlefield, and the combat itself was sometimes constrained. India's and Pakistanis are able to limit the intensity of war might and this shows a willingness to pledge not to attack population centres in a conflict. Mutual security pledges are inherently uncertain, but if established on a commonly held perception, they might gain greater weight. To the extent that the two sides accept a minimal deterrence posture, then a no-population centers pledge could reinforce both sides sense of security during a crisis. This can decrease the likelihood of war, as it can allow more time for negotiations, cooling off mediation and diplomacy.
2. Agreement on Chemical Weapons: This declaration is, therefore, a in effect a pledge not to produce chemical weapons. It is certainly a salutary step, and as with any security pledge, it lacks verification provisions. It may be

that this is a pledge, which both sides can easily make because neither has any plans to develop or field chemical weapons. Even if this agreement fits the common complaint that arms control is possible only where it is unnecessary, and impossible where it is needed, it is precisely the kind of small step that needs to be taken for confidence about the other sides intentions to take hold.

3. Covert or Overt Nuclear Posture: Nuclear ambiguity has given diplomatic flexibility to both India and Pakistan in dealing with nuclear issues at home and abroad or that a form of "non weaponized nuclear deterrence" developed between India and Pakistan. This argument assumes, that the current non proliferation regime will remain in perpetuity and that South Asia's nuclear posture will be carefully managed. It should not be impossible to separate the question of the de-jure nuclear weapons status for India's and Pakistan's nuclear capabilities. But in both, India and Pakistan, there is continuing reluctance to come to terms with the need for India and Pakistan to acknowledge each other's nuclear capabilities and initiate a dialogue aimed at learning to live in deployment or non-deployment of nuclear weapons, negotiating CSBMs for the prevention of war in general, and crisis management in particular.

4. From Tacit to Explicit Bargaining: The current state of relations between India and Pakistan should not lead us to ignore the long record of bilateral negotiation and problem solving between the two countries. Some events including the destruction of the Babri Masjid, the communal riots in Bombay, and the Charar-e-Sharief fiasco, have disrupted the dialogue. The transformation of the domestic situations in both countries, marked by the rise of religious right and the hardening of popular animosities between the two nations, make it necessary to open up and institutionalize the negotiation of CSMBs.

The United States have now begun to emphasize war - avoidance. It is also urging India and Pakistan to initiate a direct high-level dialogue on the nuclear issue. Washington formally outlined a detailed agenda on nuclear and non - nuclear CSMBs for India and Pakistan to consider. The proposal includes measures that will cap nuclear capabilities in the region, introduce a nuclear restraint regime, prevent war and generate transparency. There have been a number of unofficial proposals detailing possible CSBMs for the subcontinent. Our concern here is with only those measures that relate to crisis management. These measures can be unilateral, bilateral or multilateral.

5. Preventing Preemptive Strikes: The agreement not to attack each other's nuclear facilities has been an important CSBM that has effectively reduced the fears of nuclear preemption on the subcontinent. The agreement mandate that each country provides the other with a list of the latitudes and longitudes of its covered nuclear installations and facilities at the beginning of every year and whenever any changes are made.

Other measures to reduce prospects for preemption might include dispersal of forces, mobility, hardening and improving readiness levels. It will be prudent for both countries to decide not to keep all their special nuclear material in one place. Neither country is in such a position as to be overly apprehensive about all its delivery systems being wiped out in a single preemptive strike by the other. Nevertheless, both might consider hardening the shelters of their nuclear strike aircraft, and both may deploy mobile missiles. Improving readiness levels will tend to loosen control over nuclear forces and may be unnecessary for India and Pakistan.

6. Crisis Communication: Effective signaling and communication during a crisis can be improved by strengthening the existing communication channels and instituting new ones. There are suggestions for a similar mechanism (DGMOs) between the chiefs of air operations in the two air forces. Though there is a need for upgrading and modernizing the existing DGMO hotline, and for establishing additional ones. It may be the establishment

of crisis management groups at the appropriate levels to ensure not only that incidents and accidents that have potential to escalate and at once bring to the notice of the other side, but also that decisions get made quickly enough to defuse the situation. Decision making in India, involves a number of institutions and bureaucracies and the political leadership at the highest level. Crisis management groups with the right authority may be able to quicken the path of decision-making. Effective crisis management groups would have to involve the military services, civilian defence officials, and diplomats. Establishing risk reduction centers, on both sides, can be one way of putting together responsible crisis management teams.

7. Preventing Loss of Control: If the spread of nuclear weapons cannot be stopped, it may be a good policy to mitigate the dangers associated with nuclear weapons. New Delhi and Islamabad can begin to strengthen the physical security and safety of their nuclear materials and facilities. They can also unilaterally work toward improving other elements of managing their incipient nuclear forces such as command and control or safe storage issues.

8. Joint Military Commissions: Expanding the exchange between India and Pakistan can be a useful measure for managing crisis. The interaction between these two countries should involve, not only the discussion of military doctrine and regular high level visits, but also establishment of a joint military commission charged with periodically reviewing dangerous military activities and incidents, as well as procedures for defusing them. The establishment must be modest due to political tension between these two countries. That brings us back to the basic paradox of arms control. It is least feasible politically when it is most needed to avoid war, and it is relatively easy to accomplish when political relations are not hostile.

India and Pakistan are now on the verge of undergoing a similar learning process. The outcome remains to be seen, but the evidence assembled suggests that the risks of nuclear war in South Asia can be controlled, if India and Pakistan effectively apply arms control and aforesaid confidence building measures to their emerging nuclear relationship.

In this regard, the USA will have to shoulder greater portion of responsibility as the sole super power of the world and champion of the causes of democracy and peace.

Increasing trends of liberalization and globalization the world over add many new dimensions to the already complex problem of too many facets called "peace". If we want to save humanity from devastation and destruction that a war brings, and there is no denying the fact that we have to join hands to build and strengthen and enhance the confidence building measures in all the regions of turmoil, not only in South Asia, and the USA cannot shrug away from the responsibilities it has to share in this noble task.

Reference

1. Pakistan Warns of Another War, Indian Express, January 18, 1994, p. 8.
2. Singh Sampooran, India and the Nuclear Bomb. (1971), p. 170.

Appendix-1

Opinion
Benazir's Detente Plan

K.S. Bajpai

A really significant route to Indo-Pakistan harmony was outlined in the New York Times by Ms. Benazir Bhutto. Never mind that underlying it is the same Pakistani objective of changing the status of Kashmir with India, or that its comparison with the Arab-Israel 'peace process' (apparently inspired by a chance Berkeley encounter with Shimon Peres) is unsustainable, or even that it is in essence the approach India has always urged: improve relations in other fields, then talk about Kashmir. The temptation to argue such points must not come in the way if a new ray, or at least glimmer, of light has at last been cast from a Pakistani perspective on an otherwise dismal scene. Dare one also see in it a glimmer of hope.

Ms. Bhutto regrets "holding Indian-Pakistani relations hostage to the single issue of Kashmir", and now proposes "soft borders" and other aids to fraternization between the divided people of the State, not only for their sake, but to help the two countries initiate constructive intercourse. Her most interesting proposal is that, simultaneously, the barriers built up between the two countries should also give way - to free trade, economic cooperation, cultural, educational and people-to-people exchanges.

Very sensibly, she envisages the unfreezing of relations with India as part of South Asian cooperation. What an irony! After partition, every part of a once single economic and functional, if not legal, entity, strove to undo all the commonalities they had jointly enjoyed. To illustrate the disarray to which we all deliberately reduced ourselves: until recently, you could not phone Delhi from Lahore, except via London or Tokyo. SAARC till now was largely rebuilding the infrastructure of interaction we had inherited and discarded: postal services, communication links, flood warnings and locust control. The greatest obstacle to any substantial regional cooperation has been the endless bickering between its two most powerful constituents fuelled mainly by that element in Pakistan, which has always insisted that there could be no normalization without Kashmir.

Which is where we all, including Ms Bhutto, must take heed. She particularly, knows that the biggest enemy of what she proposed is the group in her own country which brought down her father, and then her, and which engineers stunts like Kargil to maintain hostility with India. Of course, we Indians are no angels and certainly should not expect to be so viewed. Nevertheless, in this case we have no interest in rocking any boat we are the status quo power.

The challenge to the status quo is two-fold: Kashmiri dissatisfactions and Pakistani ambitions. The latter have always been containable as long as the Valley acquiesced in the Indian nexus. Past mismanagement by politicians in Delhi, unbelievably oblivious of the extraordinary sensitivities involved in this unique relationship, gave Pakistan the opportunity to work its mischief. When at long last Delhi seemed to be getting another chance to work out its equations with the people of the state, Pakistan's hardliners had to find new means to destabilize the situation.

The others in Pakistan have reached the conclusions now given the weight of Ms Bhutto's advocacy, that it has encouraged some Indians to suppose the bad old day can be buried in history. Can such moderate and realistic Pakistanis ever prevail against the Gang of Four irreconcilables the military mavericks, the mullahs, that part of the Punjabi hierarchy that relies on perpetual tension with India, and the politicians (such as one we need not here name) who choose to connive with the other three to arouse a susceptible public?

Ms Bhutto would surely deny any adaptation of India's position, from which it does have this vital difference: it envisages a major re-arrangement between Pakistan-held Kashmir and the India side. Some leading Indian opinion makers have long urged turning Kashmir, the major area of discord, into an instrument of friendship. Such sweet reasoning conjures up pretty pictures, but obscures reality. Except for the tragically divided families, unhappiness with India among the Kashmiri-speaking Valley people is hardly caused by their inability to interact with their "brethren" across the LOC. One cannot attribute even emotional homogeneity to the complex ethnic mix that came under one dynasty's rule, or forget the deep misgivings in the Valley about the harshness associated with the "Kashmiri's" on the Pakistani side. To argue that the hodgepodge called Jammu and Kashmir State wants to be one again, is an obvious weapon for independence advocates, but it has no substance. Still, opening up old links would be worth serious thought if it helped get Pakistan on the right course.

India's difficulty is that whereas it simply may work out some new ways to make the people of the Valley feel confident of a future in India, there is nothing that can be given to Pakistan. In a perverse sense, the Pakistani mischief-makers are right: they cannot get what they want any other way. What they refuse to learn is that they cannot get it their way either, partly because they persist in the arrogant illusion that we are weaklings and partly because, with out own easy-going habits, we have failed to make the real lesson indisputable. The sad probability is that even if they did learn, they would be all the more committed to their hard line since they thrive on negativism.

In any case, until Pakistan's power structure can re-shape itself to reduce their role to manageable proportions they will remain the force that people like the present Bhutto and we India's will both have to contend with.

Adding "betrayal of the cause" to other charges against her, Pakistan will doubtless scuttle Ms. Bhutto's suggestion straightaway. Any welcome from us will work further against her, but the welcome is due. It will do no good to claim we have always thought on the same lines, but insofar as there is genuine anxiety in the world that Indo-Pakistan tensions can set out of hand, we must isolate and project the role of Pakistan's intransigence in doing precisely what Ms. Bhutto wants to get away from, making normalization a hostage to Kashmir and Pakistani anti-Indianism. There is still no reason to fear nuclear escalation, as all Pakistanis want the world to do, but if any would be go-gooders feel inclined to intervene, we can constructively and effectively sustain Ms. Bhutto views as the best, indeed only, approach to tranquility in our region.

In Pakistan's foreseeable politics nobody can expect Mr. Benazir Bhutto's thoughts to help. Her appeal to the world to take note should rather be taken as an appeal for reason among her own people, and that is something we can all urge that world to encourage.

Appendix-2

Statement of Government of Pakistan on CSBMs between Pakistan and India

S. Shafqat Kakakhel

On May 28, 1990, the Government of India conveyed to the Government of Pakistan a two page document entitled "Confidence Building Package between India and Pakistan." On June 5, 1990, the Government of Pakistan responded to India that, while it had reservations on the scope of the proposals, it was ready to engage in a purposeful dialogue and suggested that the foreign secretaries of the two countries meet that month at a mutually convenient venue to "be gin a discussion to remove the causes of the present tension". New Delhi agreed, and the first session of talks between the foreign secretaries was held in July 1990, in Islamabad. These talks have served as the main forum for negotiating confidence and security-building measures (CSBSs).

During the period July 1990 - August 1992, Pakistan and India negotiated and signed three CSBM agreements, ratified an earlier one, and held detailed discussions on several others. These discussions marked the unfolding of a structured process that has been inspired by, and to a large extent modeled on, the provisions of the Helsinki Accord and the CSBMs finalized at Madrid (1983) and Stockholm (1986) and with the Vienna Document of 1990. It should be mentioned, however, that efforts by Pakistan and India to evolve what would today be called CSBMs actually predate the U.S. -Soviet and European processes. Moreover, for reason that will be discussed later, the East-West and U.S. - Soviet models cannot be replicated in the South Asian context.

This statement will describe the progress achieved by Pakistan and India in negotiating a series of CSBM agreements, assess the significance and usefulness of these agreements and will conclude by pinpointing the inadequacies of the arrangements already in place in promoting "confidence' and 'security' between Pakistan and India. Ideally, the CBMSs in question would be studied within a historic narrative of the evolution of Indo-Pakistani relations since 1947. In view of the limitation of space and, more important in the interest of greater conceptual clarity, the process will be described and analyzed according to the categories defined by Ted Greenwood, namely, mutual security pledges transparency, managing dangerous and potentially dangerous military activities and crisis management.

Mutual Security Pledges

In 1949, soon after the first Indo-Pakistani war over Jammu and Kashmir, and amid the preoccupation of the two countries with resolving problems such as the sharing of river and canal waters and the treatment of minorities, a correspondence began between the Indian and Pakistani prime ministers, Jawaharlal Nehru and Liaquat Ali Khan. The subject of the correspondence was Nehru's proposal for a joint declaration to 'condemn (the) resort to war for the settlement of any existing or future disputes between (India and Pakistan)', and, instead, to pledge to resolve such disputes by "reorganized peaceful methods, such as negotiations, mediation arbitration, or by agreed reference to some appropriate international body recognized by both (countries)." Initially, Prime Minister Khan questioned the usefulness of what he called "a rather unnecessary repetition of certain portions, of the UN Charter". However, in a letter to Nehru, dated February 14, 1950, Khan proposed that the declaration should be supplemented by an agreement containing" a clear-cut procedure with an agreed timetable which would make it binding on both to carry out the settlement of the disputes to a peaceful conclusion." Khan further proposed that disputes be taken up one by one and' resolved through negotiation, mediation, or arbitration. He also promised that Pakistan would be willing mediation, or arbitration. He also promised that Pakistan would be willing for to accept the verdicts of a single, jointly nominated arbitrator on all bilateral disputes. Prime Minister Nehru did not accept Khan's proposal, however.

In both conceptual and political terms, the Pak-India Agreement on bilateral Relation," signed at Simla on July2, 1972, and generally referred to as the Simla Accord, constitutes a bilateral statement of mutral security pledges. The agreement declares to resolve of the two countries to "put an end to the conflict and confrontation' marring their relations and to "settle their differences by peaceful means, mutually agreed upon. "The two countries agreed not to use force to settle the situation. Paragraph 6 of the Simla Agreement reinforces these security pledges by identifying the major problem. resolved to be amicable through negotiations: the status of Jammu and Kashmir. Unfortunately, the negotiations on Kashmir envisaged in the Simla Agreement never took place. Both countries reiterated their divergent substantive positions on the disputed state: India claimed Jammu and Kashmir constituted an integral part of its sovereign territory, while Pakistan asserted that the final status of Kashmir had to be resolved in accordance with the U.N. Security Council resolutions as well as in the spirit of Simla Agreement.

Continued differences over Jammu and Kashmir did not prevent the two countries from exploring additional mutual security pledges. In September 1981, Pakistan proposed to India "consultations for exchanging mutual assurances of non-aggression and non-use of force". After receiving a positive response from New Delhi, Pakistan presented a draft non-aggression pact in June 1982. In turn, in August 1982, India proposed a draft treaty of "peace, friendship, and cooperation." After protracted negotiations, the two sides agreed in May 1984, to integrate the two drafts in to one document, entitled "Agreement / Treaty on Good Neighborliness and Cooperation." However, the Indian Government insisted that the text include a clause disallowing recourse to any third-party settlement procedure of to any international agency. India also demanded a commitment that neither country would offer military bases to a third country. Pakistan's rejections of these proposals led to yet another stalemate, and discussion on the agreement were interrupted in 1986. Prime Minister Benazir Bhutto, in a statement dated December 3, 1988, categorically opposed the idea of a new bilateral agreement, arguing that the Simla Agreement provided an adequate framework for bilateral relations.

Transparency

Both India and Pakistan have large standing armies and they frequently conduct exercises. The need for a measure of transparency in these exercises should have been evident, given the conflictual nature of the bilateral relationship. Yet the subject appears not to have become salient until October 1986, when India disclosed plans for holding the largest military exercises in its history, code-named "Brasstacks IV". Pakistan sought further information about Brasstacks and proposed that the countries discuss the exchange of advance information about troop movements and military exercises. In November of the same year, Pakistani Prime Minister Mohammed Khan Junejo reiterated the proposal for "mandatory procedures for prior notification of troop movements to prevent mutual misperceptions and apprehensions in further" at a meeting with Indian Prime Minister Rajiv Gandhi. But although Gandhi promised information about Brasstacke, he did not respond directly to Junejo's proposal for a bilateral agreement on prior notification of troop movements.

The Indian government did not fulfil Rajiv Gandhi's promise. In mid-November 1986, Indian newspapers reported that a total of 250,000 army, navy, and air force troops would participate in the exercises in the Sindh-Rajasthan and Punjab sectors. By the end of November, more than 50,000 Indian troops had been deployed in the Punjab. In response, Pakistan began to deploy its troops into the Punjab as well as in Sindh / Rajasthan.

On January 23, 1987, the Indian government asked Pakistan to withdraw to peacetime locations of the forces it had deployed in the Punjab. Furthermore, Delhi warned that if Pakistan did not withdraw its troops, India would move its troops "into defensive position." That same day, the Indian government announced that forward deployment of troops in the Punjab had already commenced, and added that if Pakistani forces did not redeploy, Indian forces would also take up positions in Rajasthan and Jammu and Kashmir. This threat caused much anxiety in Pakistan; the outbreak of hostilities appeared imminent. On January 24, Pakistan declared its readiness to hold immediate consultations to reduce the tension. India agreed the next day. On January 26, the prime ministers agreed in a telephone conversation that a Pakistani delegation would visit New Delhi. That delegation headed by the foreign secretary and comprising senior military officials, reached New Delhi on January 30.

On January 30, the Indian newspaper "The Hindu" carried a report by G.K Reddy, a senior journalist to whom that Indian government often leaked information that it did not want to disclose officially. Reddy's report stated that India wanted to "concentrate on the more immediate task of withdrawals by the two armies to their normal position," and added that Pakistan realized that India would not at the stage and forum discuss issues like a balanced reduction of forces, procedures for exercises, and posting of observers on the prevailing pattern in Europe between NATO and Warsaw Pact forces".

At the talks, Pakistan pointed out that the tense situation could have been avoided if India had provided information about the military exercises. Pakistan proposed several measures to improve communication and effect transparency, including restraints on the introduction of additional troops daily direct communications between the directors-general of military operations regular contact between the foreign ministries avoidance of flights by military aircraft, and timetables for the phased redeployment of troops. In view of the anticipated negative response from the Indian side, Pakistan did not formally introduce the proposal it had drawn up for an institutionalized system of prior notification of exercises and other military movements.

On February 4, 1987, an agreement was finally reached on the de-escalation of tension through several measures, especially the establishment of "hotline' communications between the army and air force operations chiefs to "prevent misconceptions, hasty reactions, and unfortunate incidents at a time when large numbers of forces have been deployed on the two sides of the border". This de-escalation agreement helped to disperse the clouds of war hove ring on the horizon.

Significantly, the U.S. government promptly and warmly welcomed this agreement. In identical messages delivered to the Pakistani and India governments by the U.S. ambassadors in Islamabad and Delhi, Washington recalled that it had provided information on exercise notification procedures in effect in Europe to both countries in the fall of 1986, and expressed belief that "such procedures might have helped prevent the recent escalation of tensions. "Further, Washington offered help" in ways both (countries) deem useful."

In the next two years, Indo-Pakistani relations were marred by sustained Indian accusations that Pakistan was encouraging and abetting the Sikh insurgency in Punjab by giving arms, training, and sanctuary to Sikh militants. Pakistan denied the charges and suggested that the interior secretaries of the two countries meet to discuss measures to halt illicit and undesirable border crossing. India agreed and several rounds of talks were held.

Other contentious problems between the two countries included the withdrawal of forces from the Siachen Glacier, where Indian forces had made incursions in 1984; India's construction of a navigation and water storage project (The Wullar Barrage / Tulbul Navigation Project) near Srinagar in Kashmir, which in Pakistan's view violated the Indus Waters Treaty of 1960; India's tacit support for the Soviet military intervention in Afghanistan; and New Delhi's hue and cry over Pakistan's nuclear program and its acquisition of military hardware for Washington. Despite these problems, however, the two countries maintained "normal" relations through regular high-level exchanges facilitated by SAARC, secretary-level talks on Siachen and on the Wullar Barrage Project, and meetings of the bilateral Joint Ministerial Commission. Prime Minister Rajiv Gandhi visited Islamabad for the SAARC summit in December 1988, and paid an official bilateral visit in July 1989. These high-level exchanges generated much optimism about a gradual improvement in relations and peaceful settlement of the outstanding problems, especially Siachen and Wullar Barrage.

Yet, although there were hopes of improvement in Indo-Pakistani relations the situation in Jammu and Kashmir was heading downhill. In 1989 anti-Indian demonstrations, spearheaded by Kashmiri youth in Srinagar became a recurring feature. Kashmiri Muslims refused to take part in the Indian general election. The Indian authorities tried to stem the demonstrations by force, which only caused the militants to stop up their disruptive actions. The crackdown in occupied Jammu and Kashmir was accompanied by a vigorous government propaganda campaign portraying the uprising as having been provoked and sustained by Pakistan. New Delhi also started deploying troops along the line of control and near the international border. Pakistan in turn deployed forces and an "eyeball to eyeball" confrontation ensued. Fearing that the spiraling tension could lead to premeditated or inadvertent hostilities the Pakistani foreign minister, Sahabzada Yaqub Khan, while visiting Delhi for SAARC discussions called on Indian leaders to defuse the situation and enter into a dialogue to resolve the Jammu and Kashmir problem and all other outstanding issues. He called for the redeployment of troops to peacetime locations. Khan forcefully rejected Indian accusations of Pakistani support for the Kashmiri militants and asserted that the Kashmiri uprising was an indigenous, widespread, popular movement aimed at securing the right of self-determination pledged in U.N. Security Council resolutions. The two countries took sharply divergent positions, and Yaqub Khan's mission failed.

The foreign ministers met again in New York on April 25, but failed to bring about an improvement in the climate. On May 10, Indian Prime Minister V.P. Singh deliverd a speech in Parliament calling on the people of India to "steel their nerves" and "psychologically prepare" themselves for war.

The rising level of hostile rhetoric prompted the U.S. government to undertake a highly visible initiative to reduce tensions. Robert Gates visited Pakistan and India as a special presidential envoy. Gates arrived in Islamabad on May 19 and flew to New Delhi the next day. In meetings with senior political and military officials in both countries, Mr. Gates conveyed Washington's concern over the heightened tensions and called for immediate steps to reduce them. He proposed a "removal of deployments" and suggested that the two countries begin discussions and confidence- and security-building measures. He specifically mentioned CSBMs on prior notification of military exercises - a moratorium on military exercises at first, and subsequent holding of exercises away from the Indo-Pakistani border. He also suggested talks on the establishment of 'cautionary zones" "military -free zones", joint border patrolling, and meetings between military official. The Gates mission had a positive impact: the CSBM "package" proposed by New Delhi to Pakistan on May 23, 1990, included most of the suggestion made by Gates.

The importance of transparency in the Indo-Pakistani context is indicated by the fact that the first three proposals in the Indian CSBM package pertained to "sharing in information regarding military exercises,..... communications between military commanders....., (and) exchange of delegations of the armed forces." At the first round of talks between foreign secretaries, Pakistan presented a formal proposal on prior notification of exercises. At the second session of talks, India came US with a counter-draft. After detailed discussions between August 1990 and April 1991, an agreement on "Advance Notice of Military Maneuvers and Exercises" was signed. The instruments of ratification were exchanged during the sixth round of foreign secretary talks in August 1992. The agreement provides for advance notices on exercises, maneuvers and troop movements by army, navy, and air forces "in order to prevent any crisis due to misreading of the other side's intentions." It forbids holding of exercises in close proximity to one another, or near the border and the line of control. It contains details concerning the size, type 1 level, location, duration etc. of exercises and provisions for addressing situations caused by any changes in the schedule, size, or location of exercises.

The second proposal in India's CSBM package called for "close communications between military commanders" of sectors jointly identified during mutual consultations. This proposal was meant to formalize the bilateral agreement of February 4, 1937, to establish "hotline" communications between operation chiefs of the army headquarters. During discussion, India proposed a multi-channel system extending the hotline facilities to air force and navy establishments, and also suggested the signing of a "memorandum of understanding" to institutionalize the procedures.

The third proposal in the India package called for "mutually acceptable understandings regarding exchanges of armed forces delegations from time to time". This was a precedent setting suggestion because such exchanges, has seldom taken place in the past. Pakistan responded positively and sent a high level delegation to Delhi for five-day visit in March and April 1991. An Indian delegation visited Pakistan in September 1991. The visits helped in finalizing CSBM agreements on prior notice of military exercises, the prohibition of attack on nuclear installations, and measures to prevent violations of airspace by military aircraft.

In August 1992, during the sixth round of talks between the foreign secretaries, the Indian government formally invited the chief of army staff of Pakistan to visit India. The Pakistani army chief responded that while Pakistan was in principle not opposed to the visit, it felt that the visit should take place within the context of the overall relationship. Moreover, he said the visit should have a specific purpose and facilitate talks on specific issues rather than become a "ceremonial affair" These statements were later reiterated by the Pakistani foreign secretary.

Managing Dangerous and Potentially Dangerous Military Activities

During the visit of Pakistani President Zia-ul-Huq to India in December 1985, he and Indian Prime Minister Rajiv Gandhi agreed to conclude a bilateral agreement disallowing attacks on nuclear installations. The agreement was evidently prompted by press reports in 1934 about Indian plans for a strike against Pakistani nuclear facilities. At the time, Pakistan had warned that such an attack would trigger an all-out war. After detailed discussions an "Agreement on the Prohibition of Attack Against Nuclear Installations and Facilities was signed during Prime Minister Gandhi's visit to Islamabad in December 1988.

The second CSBM to manage dangerous and potentially dangerous military activities was the "Agreement between Pakistan and India on Prevention of Air space Violations was for Permitting Over flights and Landings by Military Aircraft", which was signed in April 1991. This agreement had been suggested by India as part of its CSBM package of May 23, 1990. Pakistan introduced a draft of the agreement at the first round of talks between the foreign secretaries. The Indian counter-draft was introduced during the second round of talks. The text was finalized during the third round and the agreement was concluded in April 1991, during the fourth round of talks. Ratification documents were exchanged during the sixth session of talks between the foreign secretaries, in August 1992. The agreement provides for measures to prevent air violations and calls for agreement provides for measures to prevent air violations and calls for communications and prior notice of aerial survey and supply dropping, for mercy and rescue missions between the air force establishments, and for measures to promote safety of air operations.

The "Joints Declaration on the Complete Prohibition of Chemical Weapons", signed by the foreign secretaries on August 19, 1992, is the third CSBM for managing dangerous and potentially dangerous military activities. This agreement disallows the manufacture, import, deployment, and use of chemical weapons. The bilateral declaration preceded the international Chemical Weapons Convention in Geneva. During the sixth round of talks between the foreign secretaries, Pakistan also proposed a bilateral agreement prohibiting the acquisition, production, deployment, and use of biological weapons on the pattern of the declaration on chemical weapons.

In Pakistan's view, an early solution of the Siachen Glacier issue would not only help avoid further human and financial losses, but would also settle a "potentially dangerous military activity", thus promoting confidence. India's large-scale operation in the area in April 1984, which enabled it to·seize big chunks of high altitude areas located near the northern areas of Pakistan, inevitably prompted the latter to move its troops into position on its side of the glaciers. This was the first "dangerous military activity" between the two countries since the East Pakistani Bangladesh war of 1971. During the past ten years, both sides have lost hundreds of troops and spent millions of dollars stressing their competing claims on an area of doubtful military significance. Most of the human losses have been caused by the inhospitable terrain and punishing weather conditions at altitudes raining between 10,000 and 22,000 feet above sea level.

In January 1986, at Pakistan's suggestion, the defense secretaries of Pakistan and India began talks to resolve the Siachen problem. Both countries agreed on the desirability of an early agreement on the withdrawal and redeployment to troops and subsequently on precisely demarcating the line of control. However, India insisted that the demarcation reflect the positions occupied in 1934, a demand that was unacceptable to Pakistan. In June 1939, the defense secretaries agreed that both countries would redeploy their forces to positions to be jointly identified by their military experts. The agreement announced in a joint press statement seemed to reflect the thaw in relations effected by Prime Minister Rajiv Gandhi's visit to Pakistan in December 1939; it was endorsed by Prime Ministers Gandhi and Benazir Bhutto during the former's second visit to Islamabad in July 1939. However, controversy arose on the interpreation of the agreement Pakistan stated that the agreement would result in the restoration of the status quo prior to the incursion of Indian troops in 1934. This statement was contested by India. Further talks between military officials in August 1939s did not achieve any positive result. Subsequently, New Delhi's position hardened. In discussions between the foreign secretaries during 1990-92, New Delhi insisted that the redeployment of forces and determination of new positions must be based on the "new realities" a euphemism for positions occupied by it in 1934.

At the sixth round of talks between the foreign secretaries in August 1992, the Indians called for a meeting between defense secretaries and promised a more flexible attitude. When this meeting took place in November 1992, however, India reiterated the demand for an acknowledgment by Pakistan of the "New realities". The talks ended in failure.

Although no major military encounter has taken place in the Siachen Glacier zone, there is always the potential for clashes and conflict. Pakistan believes that an early decision on redeployment of forces would not only save precious human lives financial resources and military hardware, but would also serve as an effective confidence-and security-building measure.

Since the Indian nuclear explosion of 1974, which heralded the advent of the nuclear era in the sub-continent, Pakistan has ceaselessly worked for nuclear nonproliferation in South Asia. Its proposal for a nuclear free zone in the region enjoys the support of a large number of countries in the United Nations. At the bilateral level, Islamabad has made seven proposals:

1. Simultaneous accession by India and Pakistan to the Nuclear Nonproliferation Treaty (NPT);
2. Simultaneous acceptance by both countries of full-scope IAEA safeguards;
3. A joint declaration renouncing the acquisition of development of nuclear weapons;
4. Establishment of a nuclear-weapons-free zone in South Asia;
5. A bilateral treaty banning all nuclear tests;
6. Convening of a conference on nuclear nonproliferation in South Asia under U.N. auspices, with participation of all regional parties; and,
7. A regional conference on nuclear nonproliferation in South Asia, to be attended by Pakistan, India, the United States, Russia and China (proposed by Pakistan in June 1991).

India has thus far turned down all these Pakistani proposals, saying that nuclear proliferation is a global problem that can only be addressed at the global level. In New Delhi's view, the NPT is a discriminatory treaty meant to perpetuate the positions of the nuclear" haves" and have notes" and it cannot serve the cause of universal nuclear disarmament. India also asserts that Pakistan's proposals are "India-centered", and do not address India's concerns regarding China and the Central Asian states which are brimming with nuclear arms.

Recently, the United States, Canada, Japan and the countries of the European Union have made concerted effort to prevent nuclear weapons and missile proliferation in South Asia. Washington has reportedly suggested that Pakistan and India consider a CSBM regime that would preclude the acquisition and deployment of ballistic missiles. The U.S. government has imposed sanctions against Pakistan and China in retaliation for alleged missiles transfers from Beijing to Islamabad, which Washington claims violated the Missile Technology Control Regime. China and Pakistan deny the U.S. change, arguing that it is based on flawed information.

Crisis Management and Conflict Resolution

Since the start of the bilateral discussions on CSBMs in July 1990, Pakistan has expressed the view that the process of building, sustaining, and promoting confidence and security between Pakistan and India would require much more than the various agreements for conflict avoidance aimed at bringing about greater transparency in the actions of the armed forces. Islamabad believes that the two countries should go beyond the avoidance and containment of crisis and summon the necessary political will to expeditiously and amicably resolve the "core", "major", and "serious" issues in Indo-Pakistani relations. The core "issue is the final status of Jammu and Kashmir. The major " issue is nuclear and missile proliferation. The "serious" problems comprise aredeployment of troops in and the effective demilitarization of the Siachen Glacier; the Wullar Barrage; the demarcation of land boundaries in the Sir Creek area, which would facilitate the final demarcation of maritime boundaries; the revision of border ground rules; the joint efforts to preclude illicit cross-border movement of persons and goods.

During the foreign secretary talks Pakistan, pointed out that the efficacy of the CSBM measures being negotiated would be strengthened significantly by an early dialogue on an amicable settlement of the Kashmir problem, which has bedeviled bilateral relations for nearly fifty years. During his visit to Delhi for the sixth round of talks in August 1992, the Pakistani foreign secretary delivered to India Prime Minister Narasimha Rao a letter from Pakistani Prime Minister Nawaz Sharif proposing negotiations on Kashmir. Unfortunately, New Delhi's response has been largely negative. India does not oppose talks on

Kashmir in principle, but it has made negotiations conditional on termination of Pakistan's alleged assistance to the Kashmiri militants.

Conclusions

In practical terms, the hotline communication between the directors-general of the Pakistani and Indian armies has been useful on both sides in clarifying positions on the movement of troops. The DGMOs speak with one another at least once a week- more, often if either side desires to do so. The agreement on prior notice of military operations and the airspace violation agreement have also helped in averting possible difficulties. Similarly, the no-attack agreement and the chemical weapons declaration are desirable CSBMs.

Since early 1990, Indo-Pakistani relations have deteriorated to an all-time low, resulting in the indefinite postponement of the talks between the foreign, defense, and water resources secretaries. The meeting between the prime ministers of the two countries at the SAARC summit in April 1993 did not improve either the substance or the climate of bilateral relations. The India government's massive campaign to get the U.S. government to declare Pakistan a "state supporting terrorism"- which would have led to the imposition of wide-ranging, political, economic, military, and other sanctions against Pakistan - has deeply hurt the government and people of Pakistan. The Indian campaign has been seen as evidence of incorrigible, immutable hostility toward Pakistan.

The potentially dangerous state of Indo-Pakistani relations has been caused primarily by the Kashmiri struggle for self-determination. It underlines the fact that in the absence of a peaceful, just and lasting solution of the Jammu and Kashmir problems it would be virtually impossible to erect a durable edifice of constructive, tension-free, good neighbourly relations between Pakistan and India. The Indian government's refusal to enter into a dialogue with Pakistan on Jammu and Kashmir question suggests that while the CSBMs serve to avert the accidental outbreak of hostilities, they do not contain cast-iron guarantees against armed conflict resulting from unabated deterioration of relation. The absence of any substantial break through on the vital question of nuclear and missile proliferation, which is inextricably linked with the unresolved political and territorial questions is likely to undermine efforts aimed at the signing of additional military CSBMs between Pakistan and India.

Appendix-3

Statement of Government of India on Confidence-Building Measures between India and her Neighbours

The importance and content of confidence-building-measures (CBMs) in the conduct of inter-state relations has grown in recent years. The international environment has become more responsive to the contribution of CBMs in safeguarding peace and international security. While the subject has been on the agenda of UN for almost two decades, progress has often been slow, because of the fact that the regional specificities demand their own unique prescriptions.

Conceptually, building confidence amongst states implies that the conduct of states shall become more predictable thus reducing the risk of misperception while preserving each states right to maintain its legitimate security capabilities. CBMs are not a substitute for disarmament but can help create a positive political atmosphere and reduce tension. With her long-standing commitment to peaceful co-existence, India has set into motion a process of instituting CBMs with her neighboring states. India's relations with her neighbors vary in accordance with the political dynamics of each bilateral relationship, and consequently the nature of CBMs introduced in each instance are different thereby highlighting the fact that regional specificity is an essential prescriptive and CBMs are not an assembly line production item.

India's Approach

India has approached the exercise of confidence building with her neighbors with the following objective:

1. To provide an assurance of non-aggressive intent;
2. To prevent any attempt at misrepresentation of regular activities for political ends;
3 To reduce the likelihood of escalation of tensions; and
4. To create an environment for reduction of weapons through negotiations.

The history of CBMs in different parts of the world shows that progress in concluding and implementing CBMs is often slow even though the objectives may be ambitious. To overcome this hurdle, it is essential that CBMs be taken to be complementary to national security. Negotiations on CBMs must be focused, with precise mandated, and decisions have to be made on consensus with both parties on the basis of realization that implementation of such measures would enhance the collective security of all participants.

In India's experience with her neighboring states the range of CBMs appears to cover three broad categories:

1. Political: These include 'declarations of intent', discussions on security related concepts and doctrines, measures aimed at improving people-to-people contacts, and developing a broad base for bilateral relations;
2. Communications: These include the provision of communication line such as hot lines dedicated channel links, risk reduction or conflict prevention mechanisms, periodic meetings at official level to discuss issues and defuse tensions; and
3. Technical: These would include activities relating to arms limitation and transparency, i.e. prior notifications constraints on military activities in certain zones, ceiling on military equipments etc.

The following indicate the cross- section of CBMs, which are in place between India and her neighboring states.

Pakistan

Relations with Pakistan have not been smooth. With three wars having taken place between India and Pakistan in 1948, 1965, and 1971, and the Kashmir issue outstanding, relations between the two countries are characterized by a high degree of mistrust, apprehension, hostility in public statements and even violent incidents on the border. With this background, India is attempting to put into place a number of CBMs in order to;

1. improve the content of bilateral relationship, and
2. means to prevent escalation of tensions through institutionalized links including communications.

In 1983, India and Pakistan reached an agreement on the establishment of a Joint Commission between the two countries to meet annually, with a view of promoting cooperation in "the economic, trade, industrial, education, health, cultural, consular, tourism, travel information, scientific and technological fields". Subsequently, four Sub-Commissions were set up under the Joint Commission. The third meeting of the Indo-Pak Joint Commission was held in 1989. India maintains that regular meetings of the sub-Commission and Joint Commission and implementation of the cooperative activities identified by these bodies would serve to reduce mutual mistrust and provide greater people-to-people contacts among the two countries.

At the first round of the Foreign Secretary level talks in July 1990, India put forward an integrated package of CBMs. The package included CBMs in all the three categories- political, communication and technical. It provided for information-sharing on military exercises as a means of promoting transparency and reducing misapprehension, improving communications among military commanders joint border patrolling, exchanges of delegations of armed forces and at the political level, reiteration and reaffirmation, to settling disputes through peaceful means and bilateral negotiations ceasing hostile propaganda, respecting the Line of Control and refraining from acts detrimental to peaceful harmonious relations and maintenance of non-interference in each other' internal affairs.

The six rounds of Foreign Secretary level talks have focused on carrying forward elements of the CBM package and also helped formalize the Agreement on Prohibition of Attack on Nuclear Installations and Facilities signed in December 1988. The instruments of ratification of this agreement were exchanged in January 1991, and later, on January 1, 1992, India and Pakistan exchanged the lists of nuclear installations covered under the Agreement.

At the fourth round Foreign Secretary level talks, an Agreement was signed on Advance Notice on Military Exercises, Manoeuvers and Troop Movements. Also at the fourth round of Foreign Secretary level talks an Agreement between India and Pakistan was signed on 'Prevention of Air Space Violations and Permitting Over flight and Landings by Military; Aircraft". The instruments of ratifications of these two Agreements were exchanged at the sixth round of Foreign Secretary level talks. Both these Agreements will go a long way in reducing misapprehensions. Implementation experience with these Agreements will indicate the areas where additional measures will be needed.

At the fifth round of Foreign Secretary level talks, it was agreed that India and Pakistan would consider issuing a Joint Declaration of Prohibition of Chemical Weapons. Such a Declaration was issued at the conclusion of the sixth round of Foreign Secretary level task. Under this Declaration, both countries have undertaken not to develop, produce, acquire or use chemical weapons and also to refrain from assisting or encouraging others from doing so. Both countries have also reiterated their resolve to become original States Parties to the Chemical Weapons Convention being currently negotiated at the Conference on Disarmament.

Communications between the two countries have also been improved. Following the third round of Foreign Secretary level talks in December 1990, it was agreed that Director General of Military Operations of both countries shall remain in telephonic contact over the telephone hot line on a weekly basis. As a step towards transparency, a formal invitation was extended to the Chief of Army Staff of Pakistan to visit India. This invitations was conveyed during the sixth round of Foreign Secretary level talks.

With a view of taking concrete measures to contain terrorism, drug trafficking and smuggling and illicit border crossing along Indo-Pak border, it was agreed in 1989 that the DG of Pakistan Rangers and IG of BSF shall meet bi-annually to review implementation of agreements in this field in additions to maintaining the boundary pillars.

While India would have preferred a speedier implementation of these CBMs with a view to building upon them, it is clear that by their very nature, the pace of CBMs cannot be forced and must reflect genuine political will on the part of the states concerned.

Nepal

At the political level, relations between India and Nepal have been extremely close. Even though differences in the economic, trade, water sharing etc. areas, have arisen, the existence of effective and responsive institutional level exchanges and extensive contacts among the leaders, have helped in resolving these issues through peaceful means.

The Indo-Nepal Treaty of Peace and Friendship continues to provide the underpinning of the special relationship between the two countries with its provision for national treatment of Nepalese citizens in India (except for political rights), and an affirmation of shared security perceptions. This special relationship is characterized in the open border that India shares with Nepal, which gives the Nepalese citizens the right to enter India without a visa, seek employment and also enjoy rights of residence.

The Indo-Nepal relationship is characterized by frequent high-level political exchange. The gamut of bilateral relations between India and Nepal are covered under the Indo-Nepal Joint Commission, set up in 1988, with three Sub-Commissions dealing with Trade and Transit, Economic and Industrial Cooperation and Water Resources.

Bhutan

India's relationship with Bhutan falls into a special category and is governed by the 1949 Friendship Treaty. With Bhutan too, India has an open border and Bhutanese nationals have the rights to the same treatment in India (except for political rights) as Indian nationals, i.e., right to work, right to residence and right to travel freely. The relationship between India and Bhutan is characterized by frequent high level political exchanges which act as CBMs and help in resolving and outstanding issues.

China

Normalization of relations between India and China, after the 1962 conflict, has been a slow process. A new beginning was made in 1988, when Prime Minister' Rajiv Gandhi paid a goodwill visit to China at the invitation of Prime Minister Li Peng. The Joint Communique issued at the conclusion of the visit emphasized that principles of Panchsheel as guiding the conduct of bilateral relations between the two counties-mutual respect for sovereignty and territorial integrity, mutual non-aggression, non-interference in each other's internal affairs, equality and mutual benefit and peaceful coexistence".

A significant achievement of the 1988 visit was the setting up of a Joint Working Group on the boundary question and another Joint Group to deal with issues regarding cooperation in the fields of economic relations, trade,science and technology. The process of consolidation of political relationship has continued. During the visit of Premier Li Peng to India in December 1991, an Agreement was signed on the re-establishment of Consulates General in Shanghai and Bombay, a Consular Convention between the two countries was concluded and MOUs signed for the resumption of border trade. In May 1992, President Venkataraman paid a State visit to China. The joint statement at the end of the visit reflected the firm resolve of the two countries to settle the boundary question through peaceful negotiations and continue progress for enhancement of confidence building between the two countries in the border areas.

The India-China Joint Working Group on boundary issues has met four times and is also looking at technical and communication linked CBMs. At the fourth meeting in February 1992, it was agreed that military personnel of both countries would hold regular meetings in June and October at' Bumla Pass (eastern sector) and Spanggur Gap (western sector). Supporting communication links are being established in both sectors. In addition to the regular scheduled meetings, additional meetings of border personnel would be held as and when required. Discussions in the Joint Working Group have focussed on technical aspects of CBMs in the areas along the Line of Actual Control, such as prior notification regarding military exercises. In the statement released during the visit of President Venkataraman, it was noted that CBMs would contribute significantly to the creation of a favorable and positive atmosphere for an early, fair, reasonable and mutually acceptable settlement of the boundary question between the two countries.

Exchanges between the National Defence College in India and the National Defence University of China; between the Institute of Defence Studies and Analyses and Beijing Institute of Strategic Studies have provided for greater contacts and exchange of views. High-level defence visits have been exchanged between the two countries and the India Defence Minister visited China for the first time in July 1992.

Bangladesh

Indo-Bangladesh relations, despite occasional irritants, reflect shared values and common interests. Characterized at the political level by frequent high level exchanges, the institutional mechanism between the two countries effectively function to prevent any differences from escalation. The land boundary between India and Bangladesh was demarcated in May 1974, and joint guidelines were issued the following year for the border authorities, namely, the BSF and the Bangladesh Rifles. These guidelines are intended to help the two para-military organizations to tackle problems of unauthorized movement of persons, inadvertent crossing of land and riverine boundaries, smuggling, communications while in hot pursuit of criminals, curbing traffic in illicit weapons and dealing with border crimes. Significantly, the two countries have agreed that no defensive works, e.g. trenches etc. shall be permitted within 150 yards on either side of the international boundary. Annual border coordination meetings are held between the two para-military organizations with more frequent meetings at the sector and sub-sector commander levels.

Specifications for flag communications and telephone communications have been laid down to ensure reliable contact between the border security agencies.

A number of training slots are provided on a regular basis to Bangladesh defence personnel in Indian training establishments, at all level. A programme of exchange of goodwill visits has begun with the first visit of the Indian Chief of Army Staff to Bangladesh in July 1991.

A Joint Economic Commission was set up in 1932. Cultural and academic exchange programmes provide greater people-to-people contact between the two countries.

Myanmar

Despite fluctuations in Indo-Myanmar relations during the last three decades, there remain strong links of shared historical cultural and ethnic ties between the people of the two countries. As with other neighboring countries, a Treaty of Friendship was signed between India and Myanmar in 1951. Myanmar, as founder member of the Nonaligned Movement, and India, also shared common perceptions on international issues.

Agreements on delimitations of land boundary and the maritime boundary signed in 1967 and 1936 have yet to be followed through to completion.

A major political effort to improve relations was undertaken during former Prime Minister Rajiv Gandhi's visit to Myanmar in 1987. However, some of the momentum was lost due to internal developments in Myanmar demarcation, as provided for in the boundary delimitation agreement, can completed following inspections of the boundary pillars on the border.

Faced with common problem of trans-border terrorism, bilateral meetings between Area Commanders of the border security forces have been instituted. These meetings take place twice a year with the objective of exchanging information and coordinating to the extent possible, anti-insurgency operations in the border areas.

Maldives

Indo-Maldives relation have been a steady improvements since 1976 when a Maritime Boundary Agreement between the two countries was signed settling the issue of competing territorial claims over a part of Mincoy Islands. Bilateral political relation showed an upswing following the visit of former Prime Minister Rajiv Gandhi in 1986. Since then, exchange of high level visits between the two countries has continued on a regular basis.

An Indo-Maldives Joint Commissions set up in 1990, provides the framework for expanding bilateral economic and technical cooperation and improving people-to people contacts. Health, welfare, communication, human resource development, infra-structural projects are some of the areas of activity under the Indo-Maldives Joint Commission.

The strong ties between the two countries, was reflected in India's timely assistance to the Maldives Government during the 1988 crisis. Defence cooperation has also been expanded since 1988. It now includes provision of training slots in Indian establishments for Maldives defense personnel. In 1991, the practice of holding joint coastguard exercises between the services of the two countries was instituted.

Sri Lanka

Despite contentious and difficult issues relating to the Tamil refugee problem, Indo-Sri Lankan relations reflect a high degree of interaction across a broad range of issues testifying to the functioning of institutional mechanisms. A major landmark in the bilateral relationship is the Indo-Sri Lanka Agreement of July 1987, in which India is committed to the establishment of peace and normalcy in Sri Lanka with a view to preserving its character as a multi-ethnic, multi-lingual and multi-religious plural society. India has also assured Sri Lanka that its territory shall not be used for activities prejudicial to the unity, integrity and security of Sri Lanka.

The close relations between the armed forces of the two countries are promoted through the provision of a number of training slots in Indian defense training establishments for Sri Lankan officers at all levels. Close cooperation between the Navies and Coastguard forces of the two countries has been instituted to curb patching, fishing in each other's territoritorial waters, smuggling etc. The Navies of the two countries have also cooperated with regard to the repatriation of Sri Lankan refugees.

To provide broader content, an Indo-Sri-Lankan Joint Commission was established in 1991. Initially, two Sub-Commission on Trade, Investment and Finance and Social, Cultural and Educational Affairs were set up. An addition was soon made by instituting a third Sub-Commission to deal with Science and Technology. In recent years there are growing interest in looking for joint ventures in industries and services.

Conclusion

The short review of CBMs instituted between India and her neighbors in recent years reveals a wide spectrum. In a sense, it is reflection of the dynamics of the bilateral relationship in each instance. Geography also conditions the issues in each relationship. In certain cases India shares a long land boundary with its neighbors; in others there are religious, ethnic or linguistic links among populations on both sides of the international border, which creates the problem of tracking refugee movements and infiltration. A number of neighboring states are much smaller than India and special efforts are needed to provide necessary reassurances to these states guaranteeing their territorial integrity and sovereignty. With such a broad spectrum of issues, clearly CBMs need to be explored and tailor-made to suit specific requirement. Imposing a uniform pattern may be counter -productive because it is only in one-to-one discussions and negotiation that India is in a position to be able to respond to concerns animating each bilateral relationship.

Confidence must be enhanced on all fronts and in tandem, if security has to be enhanced. Political declarations are significant but these must be supported by actions that reflect a desire for just and secure peace; actions that discard the option of military solutions, overt or covert, to resolve political problems; action that reject military postures that are perceived as hostile. Continuance of hostile acts and inflammatory statements diminish the value of political CBMs. In a region where a desire for peace has taken root must demonstrate a change in priorities, reflected through increasing intercourse among institutions, among public interest groups, and among people through cultural, communication and economic linkages.

India will continue its effort to build upon the existing CBMs in a step-by-step and realistic manner. Effective implementation of existing CBMs paves the way for more steps in this direction. Once again, these would reflect a wide spectrum, depending on the political dynamics of the relationship and receptivity of the other state. From reducing misperception and improving communications, India considers it possible to visualize movement towards reducing troop deployment or establishment of 'zones of restraint'. Once political dialogue on all issues is firmly established and security perceptions undergo changes; development of closer commercial and economic ties; improving communications and travel for the people through easing restraints; further strengthening cultural links, putting into place non-discriminatory and structural measures for curbing proliferation and contribution to global elimination of weapons of mass destruction; and eventually, moving towards open exchanges of security perceptions which will lead in turn to reduction of military expenditures.

Plurality is the true test of democracy and plurality requires openness and tolerance in social policy. Accepting the concept of cooperative security and enhancing it through confidence-building measures needs political resilience based on democratic principles. India's initiatives for confidence building are rooted in the bedrock of these principles. Once a uniform degree of openness is established in each society, and range of effective bilateral institutional mechanisms are put into place, applicability of regional approach in the area of confidence-building measures will become feasible and productive. India is committed to seeking ways and means to improve its bilateral relations with all the states in its neighbourhood and shall continue assiduously to pursue appropriate CBMs in keeping with the principles of Panchsheel, which form a basis for India's conduct of inter-state-relations.

Appendix-4

A Blueprint for Peace

In September 1995, Stephen Cohen wrote to a democratic US senator, outlining his proposals for a peace process for South Asia. The following are excerpts from the letter.... .

1. The process must be bipartisan. If you go to the president, it should be with a respected Republican senator. Our engagement in the Middle East has been bipartisan, and has thus survived several changes in administration.

2. The process should be seen as long-haul. Like Cambodia and South Africa, as well as the Middle East, the process of building peace in South Asia will take time. There will also have to be a change in attitudes, although I believe that a new generation of leaders in the region will speed up the process.

3. Camp David-style process of negotiations should not come first. That is Carter's intense intervention took place after several years of patient diplomacy. It is important to obtain early, high-visibility presidential support- perhaps a brief meeting between prime ministers in the White House or at Camp David - but we are looking for trouble if the president (especially this president) is required to broke a deal. Neither side is reads yet, and both think they can manipulate us (especially through the Congress) without having to negotiate the president might become involve at that stage.

4. We need a special emissary, someone with time, a solid reputation in both countries as well as the ability to retain the attention of our own bureaucracy, and subordinate our diverse interests to the longer- term goal of reaching an

India-Pakistan detente. The State Department does not seem able to assume this role (frankly, no one else in the bureaucracy seems to pay any attention to them). An emissary might best be situated in the White House (where, however, there is little interest in South Asia except for the proliferation issue) or the Department of Defence. My own candidate would be George Schultz, a realist with the respect of both sides, who understands the task of consensus building (he single-handedly revived the Middle East peace process). Mike Armacost was involved as a special emissary at one time, and is another possibility, and so is the "father" of the Middle East peace process, Hal Saunders, who introduced into South Asia some of the ideas he developed for the Middle East.

5. South Asia peace process will not be expensive (except in terms of time). Unlike the Middle East, where there has been a great deal of aid, in South Asia we should not emphasize military assistance, but rather technical aid and economic investment. Our best argument is that a peaceful region is one where American investors will put their money and that in the long run, this is the best assurance of regional progress.

   Congress can influence events positively. Congress will have to present a united front to both India and Pakistan, as each tries to undercut the other in whatever way they can. I like the idea making a deal conditional on progress towards regional discussions.

6. An American "helping hand" (not a "foreign hand") will be welcome in India, despite the apparent opposition of the present government. The Indians know they are in deep trouble in Kashmir, and do not want to alienate the US. Thoughtful Indians also realize that in the long run, it is in their interest to cooperate with Pakistan. There is support for a fair, consistent and long-term American effort to assist the two countries, so they can get down to the more important tasks of economic development and social change.

Appendix-5

The Lahore Declaration

The Prime Ministers of the Republic of India and the Islamic Republic of Pakistan:

Sharing a vision of peace and stability between their countries, and of progress and prosperity for their people.

Convinced that durable peace and development of harmonious relations and friendly cooperation will serve the vital interests of the people of the two countries, enabling them to devote their energies for a better future.

Recognizing that the nuclear dimension of the security environment of the two countries adds to their responsibility for avoidance of conflict between the two countries.

Committed to the principles and purposes of the Charter of the United Nations, and the universally accepted principles of peaceful coexistence.

Reiterating the determination of both countries to implementing the Simla Agreement in letter and spirit.

Committed to the objective of universal nuclear disarmament and nor-proliferation.

Convinced of the importance of mutually agreed confidence building measures for improving the security environment.

Recalling their agreement of 23rd September, 1998, that an environment of peace and security is in the supreme national interest of both sides, and that the resolution of all outstanding issues including Jammu and Kashmir, is essential for this purpose.

Have agreed that their respective Governments:

1. Shall intensify their efforts to resolve all issues, including the issue of Jammu and Kashmir.
2. Shall refrain from intervention and interference in each other's internal affairs.
3. Shall intensify their composite and integrated dialogue process for an early and positive outcome of the agreed bilateral agenda.
4. Shall take immediate steps for reducing the risk of accidental or unauthorized use of nuclear weapons, and discuss concepts and doctrines with a view to elaborating measures for confidence building in the nuclear and conventional fields, aimed at prevention of conflict.
5. Reaffirm their commitment to the goals and objective of SAARC and to concert their efforts towards the realization of the SAARC vision for the year 2000 and beyond with a view to promoting the welfare of the peoples of South Asia, and to improve their quality of life through accelerated economic growth, social progress and cultural development.
6. Reaffirm their condemnation of terrorism in all its forms and manifestations and their determination to combat this menace and,
7. Shall promote and protect all human right and fundamental freedoms.

Appendix-6

Frequently Asked Questions on Jammu and Kashmir

Q 1. The Accession of Jammu & Kashmir to India is disputed and ceded to the Indian Union only the areas of defense, foreign affairs and finance. What has made India regard accession as permanent?

At the time of Independence, India was primarily under two administrations: The Government of India directly run by the British Crown; and the princely states who owed allegiance to the Crown but administered their own territories. The Accession of Jammu & Kashmir to India was made in accordance with the India Independence Act, 1947. Under this Act none of the princely states was permitted to declare independence [Sec 11 (3)]. They could opt for either India or Pakistan with the executive qualifying that geographical contiguity to either state and the predominant religion of the region would govern this option. The Nizam of Hyderabad and Nawab of Khairpur were therefore required to accede to India and Pakistan respectively. The Hindu Maharajah (ruler) of J & K in fact temporized on accession in the hope that he might win independence.

A tribal invasion from Pakistan forced him to bow to the will of the then predominant political party with a primarily local Muslim leadership and following, the National Conference led by Sheikh Mohammed Abdullah, to accede to India on the prescribed terms and conditions. This was what was done. Till the arrival of the Indian Army to the relief of the beleaguered state, it was only the volunteers of the National Conference and their predominantly Muslim supporters, who "braved death in stemming the invasion" standing between the organized military forces from Pakistan and the capital Srinagar, after the invaders had overcome the State forces at the frontier town of Muzaffarabad. Thereafter, it was the local Forest Rangers of Kashmir, mostly Muslim and seconded by the emergency government of Sheikh Abdullah, who moving "across the mountains and through the forests with incredible speed... produced the most accurate information regarding enemy (Pakistan / tribal) strengths, location and movement." (Lt. Gen. LP Gen: Slender was the Thread, Orient Longman, 1969 pp. 36 & 142).

The accession of J & K to the Indian union is not disputed. However, Pakistan is, despite this clear legal position, in occupation of one third of the state (33,000 sq. miles of a total area of 85,806 sq. miles) as a result of the invasion, which has made it the subject of dispute. Moreover, this invasion cannot be passed off as a local insurrection. The presence of Pakistan's regular troops is attested by UNCIP documents. (UNCIP First Report, S / 1100).

Q 2. Was British India not finally divided into two States, one Muslim and one Hindu? With its Muslim majority and physical contiguity, should not J & K then have logically become part of Pakistan?

It is correct that British India was divided into two States: India and Pakistan. While Pakistan was avowedly a Muslim State based on a Muslim majority, India was then and has been ever since a secular state. Besides the Radcliffe Award who divided the areas under direct British rule into those with a Muslim majority from the remaining, the future of princely states lay in the nation to which they acceded. Jammu & Kashmir was such a state and it acceded to India.

Q 3. If there is indeed no dispute regarding the State's accession to India, why did the case go before the UN?

The matter was taken before the UN at a time when India was newly emerging from a century of colonial rule and in a world just recovering from perhaps the most devastating war in history. India sought UN intervention at that time, as part of the state, which had acceded to India and was therefore India Territory was under the forcible occupation of a foreign power. The UN would then have been considered by a war weary world as the future's strongest hope for amity among nations. The only other alternative would have been to pursue the war inflicting face to face components of an army which had been but, one till yesterday, with one Supreme Commander, Field Marshal Sir Claude Auchinleck and commanders-in-Chief who were both British; General Sir Frank Messervy followed by Sir Douglas Gracey of Pakistan, and General Sir Rob Lockhart followed by General Roy Bucher of India. Many formations and units of both forces continued to commanded by British officers.

Q 4. The UN had decided in 1948 that a plebiscite be held in the State of J & K to determine its future. Although both India and Pakistan accepted the resolution, why does India now resist the idea of a plebiscite?

The UN Commission for India and Pakistan (UNCIP) resolved on 13 August 1948 that a cease-ire be declared between India and Pakistan, then at war in J & K to be followed by a truce leading to plebiscite. This resolution which was accepted by, India on 20 August 1943, was in three parts:

1. Cease-fire.
2. Pakistan to unconditionally withdraw troops tribesmen and nationals from J & K.
3. Upon notification of the withdrawal of Pakistani troops and others specified in part 11, India to withdraw the bulk of her forces retaining an adequate strength for law and order duties. Plebiscite to be then held.

   No Pakistani withdrawal has taken place to date.

Q 5. There is a special clause in the Constitution of India determining the status of J & K in the Indian Union. How

then is Jammu and Kashmir described as an "integral" part of India?

There are special provisions in the Constitution of India regarding several states e.g. Maharashtra and Gujarat (Art 371), Nagaland (Art. 371-A), Assam (Art 371-B), Manipur (Art 371-C), Andhra Pradesh (Art 371-D), Sikkim (Art. 371-D), Mizoram(Art 371-G), Arunachal Pradesh (Art. 371-H), Goa (Art. 371-I). Nor are these standard provisions, but vary with the requirement of each state. Moreover, while these are permanent provisions, Art. 370, the provision in respect of J & K state is a temporary provision, revocable or subject to modification by presidential notification issued with the concurrence of the State Assembly.

Q 6. Under the above clause Indians are not permitted to purchase immovable property in the State. Has this not deliberately nurtured separatist trends in local politics?

This clause in no way governs the purchase of property in J & K and a cursory glance at the contents will bear this out. The acquisition of property in the state is governed by the Alienation of Lands Act, adopted in the time of the Maharajah and thereafter amended to allow only Indians to own immovable property. However this property is to be acquired only by those Indians who are also state subjects, or permanent residents of the State.

This is not the only part of India where the acquisition of property is thus restricted. In all states, Union Territiories or regions so classified, only resident tribals are permitted to own property e.g. Mizoram, Nagaland, Lakshadweep, Nicobar, the Bastar region of Madhya Pradesh, the Jharkand region of Bihar etc. This has in no way nurtured separatist feelings in these states or areas.

Q 7. The general belief is that the Kashmiri populace has remained mostly disaffected from India. Why has it not been

possible for India, which claims to be among the world's freest democracies to respond effectively?

There are absolutely no grounds to assume that the Kashmiri's have remained disaffected from India since the Accession. The basis of the Accession has been discussed in answer to question No.1. After the accession there has been no persistent disaffection other than sporadic, characterizing all parts of India and remedied over time by the democratic process. There have been elections held in Kashmir since 1951 as in other parts of J & K State and in the rest of the country. Although there have been allegations of malpractices in some elections, these have not been generally upheld by the legal system. Even the most trenchant critics admit that the elections of 1977 were totally free. Secession was not an issue in that election or in any other.

Even though it is alleged that the current insurgency arose as a result of "rigging" of the 1987 election, it is nowhere claimed that secession was an issue even then. If indeed there was interference in the election process (which is in itself unsubstantiated), it could therefore have been a result only of inter-party rivalry, which would have been exposed through legal recourse, had the situation so been allowed.

It might also be borne in mind that both in 1977, and in 1983 elections, wherein the ruling party at the Center contested vigorously (in both cases the Prime Ministers campaigned personally: Mr. Morarji Desai in 1977, and Mrs. Indira Gandhi in 1983), it was the regional party that triumphed, and not the ruling party at the Center, with all the resources supposedly at its disposal.

Moreover, the present disorder relates exclusively to the Kashmiri speaking portion of the population of Jammu & Kashmir. This is the population confined to 3,600 sq. miles with a population of 3.2m (1981 census). This might be compared with 12,000 sq. miles of Jammu Division (2.7m), and Ladakh 33,000 sq. miles (133,000). The Kashmiri speaking population does not embrace the entire Muslim population of the State.

There is hardly an echo of the militancy among the people of Jammu Division (30% Muslim including Muslim majority districts of Poonch and Rajouri), except in the Kashmiri speaking Doda district, or those of Ladakh (45% Muslim including the Muslim majority district of Kargil).

Q 8. Since India has not been able to resolve this issue directly with Pakistan for so long despite resort to war, why is she not agreeable to accepting UN mediation or that of a third party?

The issue concerning Pakistan is peripheral to the main issue at present under contention, which is the military confrontation which till recently existed in the State. The political issues plaguing the State can be resolved only by mutual discussion between the peoples' representatives and the Government of India. Hence, the Government's determination to return power to the people through the electoral process.

This has been the process, which has ensured internal peace to the people of Kashmir from 1949 to 1989, despite wars with Pakistan and the fact that Pakistan's basic position regarding the State has remained unchanged which is the continued occupation of a part of the State without reduction of troops. The situation has been sought to be further worsened by promotion of terrorism within the State by Pakistan, thus repeatedly delaying efforts to carry through the electoral process and resorting democracy. Such a restoration was seen as a key element in resolving issues within the State before turning to the international issues involving Pakistan. Now that elections have been conducted and a government of the J & K people restored, we can hope for an end to the suffering of the people of Kashmir. The restoration of comparative peace in the Valley, with markets bustling and holiday makers flocking the fabled gardens give grounds for optimism, provided that there is no attempt at outside interference.

The resolution of mutual issues can best be decided by dialogue between India and Pakistan, as has been decided in an agreement signed by the Prime Minister Indira Gandhi of India and then President ZA Bhutto of Pakistan on 3 July, 1972, at Shimla (Oka Simla).

The Prime Ministers of India and Pakistan met in Colombo, Sri Lanka on July 29, 1998 during the 10th SAARC Summit. The dialogue process will continue (Prime Minister's Statement in Lok Sabha / Rajya Sabha on August 3, 1998 & Foreign Secretary's Statement on the dialogue process on July 31, 1998 in Colombo, Sir Lanka). For more on India - Pakistan Dialogue.

In response to an invitation by the Prime Minister of Pakistan, Mr. Muhammad Nawaz Sharif, the Prime Minister of India, Shri Atal Bihari Vajpayee, visited Pakistan from 20-21 February 1999, on the inaugural run of the Delhi-Lahore buts service. Prime Minister Vajpayee along with Pakistan Prime Minister Sharif waving to people gathered at the Wagah Border after crossing the border by bus in Pakistan on February 20, 1999 (External Affairs Minister's Statement in the Parliament/ Lahore Declaration / Joint Statement / MoU between India & Pakistan).

Q 9. India has stated that she is willing to discuss the issue under the Shimla Agreement. In what way will this agreement insofar as it pertains to Kashmir pave the way to a peaceful settlement?

A peaceful settlement requires two essential elements:

i) That Pakistan desist from supporting and indeed championing terrorism in J & K.

ii) That internal difficulties in the State be resolved through political dialogue, between Government and people.

Once this is achieved, remaining differences with Pakistan can be resolved through bilateral dialogue as laid down in the Shimla agreement.

Q10. There are reports from human rights groups both from within India and internationally, of widespread human

rights abuses by the security forces in J & K, particularly in the Kashmir Valley. Does this not tarnish India's image for respect for human rights? What has been Government's response?

Since the descent of the State of Jammu & Kashmir into Pakistan supported militancy in 1939, there have been allegations of human rights abuses by Indian security forces. Over the last decade, thousands have lost their lives including over 1,000 members of the security forces. The terrorists specifically targeted the press including editors of the leading Kashmiri newspapers, apart from the security forces police and the judiciary. In spite of this Government took a public stand on the issue and when complaints could be legally substantiated against government personnel, action was repeatedly taken against the offenders. In 1993, by an Act of Parliament the National Human Rights Commission was set up. The Commission, staffed by retired justices, has issued instruction booklets to security personnel, as supplements to exiting instructions on how they are to behave with civilian populations in times of disorder and respect human rights in precarious situations. Over the last five years, this Commission has been widely praised, including by the US - Government, for its very active role in investigating and following up of human rights abuses in a tough and independent manner.

A similar commission has also been set up at the State level in Jammu & Kashmir after the installation of the present State Government. Government policy is therefore clear, and mechanisms also exist for restitution. There is therefore no question of a 'deterioration' in human rights.

On the other hand, any impartial observer of the subcontinent will realise that human rights abuses in Jammu and Kashmir are the result of terrorist action, ruthlessly targeting men, women and children. The US State Department's annual report on terrorism has squarely stated that there is credible evidence of official Pakistani support for terrorism in J & K. Indeed, in the last report it specifically listed the Harkat-ul-Ansar, a Pakistan based organisation, operating in J & K, as a terrorist organization. It is an offshoot of this organization that claimed responsibility for kidnapping five foreign tourists including two Americans. One of these, a Norwegian, was brutally beheaded. One American managed to escape. The fate of the others remains unknown.

Over the last few years, it has been possible, through increasingly effective action by the security forces against the terrorists, together with political initiatives to improve security for the people. The State of Jammu & Kashmir has had Parliamentary elections as well as State elections, asserting the people's will through the ballot. However, the continuing danger posed to the people by Pakistani sponsored terrorists was brought home starkly in recent months, when three massacres specifically targeting the Hindu population of the State were perpetrated in Wandhama (January 1998 slaughtering 23 members of all Hindu families in the village, Prankote (April 1998), in which 29 Hindu were dragged from their homes to be knifed, bludgeoned and shot in cold blood, and in Chapnali (June, 1998, reported in detail in the New York Times of June 20) where 25 members of a marriage party were murdered as they rested by a wayside tea stall.

The manner of these atrocities and the evidence of witnesses attest to the fact that the killers are: mostly from outside the State of Jammu & Kashmir. Surely therefore, the prerequiste for lasting peace in the State must be a complete halt to the patronage of such criminals.

Bibliography

- Agarwal, H.O., Kashmir Problem: Its Legal Aspects, Kitab Mahal, Allahabad, 1979.
- Ahmed, Emajuddin and Kalam, Abul, eds., Bangladesh, South Asia and the World, Academic Publishers, Dhaka, 1992.
- Albright, David: Berkhouit, Frans and Walker, William, World Inventory of Plutonium and Highly Enriched Uranium 1992, SIPRI and Oxford University Press Oxford, 1993.
- Ali, Akhtar, Pakistan's Nuclear Dilemma, A.B.C. Publishing House, New Delhi, 1984.
- Amin, Tahir, Ethno-National Movements of Pakistan: Domestics and International Factor, Institute of Policy Studies, Islamabad, 1988.
- Bhatia, Shyam, India's Nuclear Bomb, Vikas, New Delhi, 1979.
- Bhutto, Zulfikar Ali, If I am Assassinated, Vikas New Delhi, 1979.
- Birdwood, Lord, Two Nations and Kashmir, Robert Hale Ltd., London, 1956.
- Bowles Chester, Promises to Keep: My Years in Public Life, 1941-68, New Delhi, 1972.
- Brands, William J., India, Pakistan and the Great Powers, Praeger, New Yord, 1972.
- Brecher, M., The Struggle for Kashmir, Oxford University Press, London, 1952.
- Brines, Russel, The Indo-Pakistani Conflict, Pall Mall Press, London, 1968.
- Brodie, Bernard, ed., The Absolute Weapon: Atomic Power and World Order, Harcourt Brace, New York, 1946.
- Bull, Hedlly, ed., Intervention in World Politics, Clarendon Press, Oxford, 1984.
- Burke, S.M., Pakistan's Foreign Policy: An Historical Analysis, Oxford University Press, Oxford, 1973.
- Callord, Keeth, Pakistan Foreign Policy: An Interpretation, New York, 1957.

- Callord, Keeth, Pakistan: A Political Study, London, 1957.
- Cantori, Lois J. and Spiegel, Steven L., The International Politics of Regions: A Comparative Approach, Prentice Hall, Englewood Cliffs N.J., 1970.
- Chakravarti, B.N., India Speaks to America, Orient Longmans, New Delhi, 1966.
- Chellaney, Brahma, Nuclear Proliferation; The US-Indian Conflict, Longman, New Delhi, 1993.
- Cheema, Pervaiz Iqbal, Pakistan Defence Policy 1947-58 Macmillan Press, London, 1990.
- Cohen, Stephen P., ed., Nuclear Proliferation in South Asia, Lancer International, New Delhi, 1991.
- Cohen, Stephen P., The Security of South Asia, Vihar, New Delhi, 1988.
- Crodesman, Anthony H., US Strategic Interests in India-Pakistan Military Balance, The English Book Store, New Delhi, 1988.
- Crunden, Robert M., Joshi Manoj and Rao, P.V.R.C., eds., New Perspective on America and South Asia, Chanakya Publications New Delhi, 1984.
- Curl, Peter V., Documents on American Foreign Relations, 1954, New York, 1955.
- Echeverse Gent, John "The State and the Poor: Public Policy and Political Development in India and united state, New Delhi, 1995.
- Dunn, Lewis A. and Kahn, Herman, Pressures or Reasons for Proliferation, Houston Institute, New York, 1976.
- Gaibraith, J.K., Ambassador's Journal: A Personal Account of Kennedy's Year, London, 1969.
- Galbraith, Peter, United States Security Interests in South Asia, Govt. Printing Office, Washington D.C., 1984.
- Ganguly, Shivaji, US Policy Toward South Asia, Vanguard, Lahore, 1988.
- Ganguly, Sumit, The Origins of War in South Asia, Vanguard Lahora, 1991.
- Glazeri, Sulochana Raghvan and Glazer, Nathan Conflicting Images India and the United States. Riverdale Company, 1991.
- Green Fred, US Policy in the Security of South Asia, New York, 1956.
- Gupta, Bhabani Sen, Nuclear Weapons: Policy Options For India, Sage, New Delhi, 1983.

- Gupta, Bhabani Sen, South Asian Perspective: Seven Nations in Conflict and Cooperation, B.R. Publishing Company, New Delhi, 1988.
- Gupta, Jyoti Bhushan Das, Indo-Pak Relations 1947-55, Ojambston, Amsterdam, 1958.
- Gupta, Sisir, Kashmir: A Study in India-Pakistan Relations, Asia Publishing House, New Delhi, 1966.
- Guyer, Maurice and Appadorai A., Speeches and Documents on the Indian Constitution, Oxford University Press, Bombay, 1957.
- Hayes, Louis D., The Impact of the US Policy on the Kashmir Conflict, The University of Arizona Press, Arizona, 1971.
- Hellman, Donald, C., ed., South Asia: The Politics of Poverty and Peace, Lexington Books, Lexington, 1976.
- Hodson, H.V., The Great Divide - Britain, India and Pakistan, Hutchinson, London, 1969.
- Jaffrey, L. Ferrasi; Knopf, W. and Madrid, L., US Arms Export Policies and Contractors, Washington, 1987.
- Jain, J.P. Nuclear India, Delhi, 1974.
- Jasani, Bhupendra, ed., Nuclear Proliferation Problem, Stockholme, 1974.
- Johnson, Alan Compbell, Mission with Mountbatten, Robert Hale Ltd., London, 1952.
- Jones Joseph, M., the Fifteen Weeks, Viking, New York 1955.
- Kamath P.M. Indo-US Relations: Dynamics of Change, New Delhi, South Asian Publication 1987.
- Kapur, Ashok, Pakistan's Nuclear Development, Croom Helm, London, 1937.
- Kennedy, Paul, The Rise and Fall of the Great Powers, Random House, New York 1987.
- Khan, Akbar, Raiders in Kashmir, Pak Publishers, Karachi, 1970.
- Kheli, Shirin Tahir, ed., US Strategic Interests in South West Asia, Praeger, New York 1982.
- Kheli, Shirin Tahir, The United States and Pakistan: The Evolution of an Influence Relationship, Praeger, New York 1982.
- Korbel, J., Dangers in Kashmir, Princeton University Press, Princeton, 1954.
- Kux, Dennis, stranged Democracies India and the United States, Sage Publications, New Delhi, 1993.

- Lakhanpal, P.L. Essential Documents and Notes on Kashmir Dispute, International Books, Delhi, 1965.
- Lamb, Alistair, Kashmir: A Disputed Legacy 1946-1990, Poxford Books, Hertford, 1991.
- Limaye, Satu P., US-India Relations: The Pursuit of Accommodation, West view press, Boulder, 1993.
- Macmillan, J. and Silver, J.M., Nuclear Development in the Asia and Pacific Region, Australian Nuclear Science and Technology Organization, Sydney, 1993.
- Malhotra, V.K., ed., Indo-US Relations in Nineties Anmol, New Delhi, 1995.
- Malik, Hafeez, ed., Dilemma of National Security and Cooperation in India and Pakistan, Macmillan London, 1993.
- Mellor, Andrew, India Since Partition, London, 1951.
- Mellor, John M., India - A Rising Middle Power, Praeger, New York, 1979.
- Menon, V.P., The Story of the Integration of Indian States Orient Longman, New Delhi, 1985.
- Menon, V.P., The Transfer of Power in India, Orient Longman, Bombay, 1957.
- Meyer, S.M., The Dynamics of Nuclear Proliferation, University of Chicago Press, Chicago, 1984.
- Modelski, George, SEATO Melbourne, 1964.
- Mohite, Dilip H. Indo-US Relations Issues Conflict and Cooperation, New Delhi, South Asian Pub., 1995.
- Morgenthau. Hans, In Defence of the National Interest, Knopf, New York, 1952.
- Nayar, Baldev Raj, American Geopolitics and India, Manohar, New Delhi, 1976.
- Neuman, S.G. and Harkavy, R.G. eds., Arms Transfer in the Modern World, New York, 1980.
- Noorani, A.G., ed., The Kashmir Question, Manktalas Bornbay, 1964.
- Northedge, F.S., ed., Foreign Policy of the Great Powers London, 1963.
- Nye, Joseph, Bound to Lead: The Changing Nature of American Power, Basic Books, New York, 1990.
- Palit, D.K. and Nambodiri, P.K.S., Pakistan's Islamic Bomb, Vikas New Delhi, 1979.

- Paranjpe, Shrikant, US Non-proliferation Policy in Action: South Asia, Sterling, New Delhi, 1987.
- Pathak, K.K. Nuclear Policy of India, Gitanjali Prakashan, New Delhi, 1980.
- Paul, Ronald A., American Military Commitments Abroad, New Brunswick, New Jersey, 1973.
- Quester, George G., American Foreign Policy: The Lost Consensus, New York, 1982.
- Raghawan, Sulochana etc., eds., Conflicting Image : India and the United States Riverdale, Maryland, 1990.
- Rajan, M.S. and Ganguly, Shivaji, Great Power Relations World Order and the Third World, New Delhi, 1981.
- Ramakant, ed., China and South Asia, South Asian Publishers New Delhi, 1985.
- Rana A.P. Four Decades of Indo-US Relations: A Commemorative Retrospective, New Delhi, Har Anand and the US Educational Foundation in India, 1994.
- Rao, Kilaru Ram Chandra, India, United States and Pakistan: A Triangular Relationship, Himalaya Publishing House, Bombay 1985.
- Rizvi, Gowher, South Asia in a Changing International Order, Sage, New Delhi, 1993.
- Rizvi, Hasan Askari, Internal Strife and External Intervention India's Role in Civil War in East Pakistan, Progressive Publishers, Lahore, 1931.
- Roseneau, James ed., International Politics and Foreign Policy: A Reader in Research and Theory, The Free Press, New York, 1969.
- Roseneau, James N., ed., World Politics: An Introduction, The Free Press, New York 1976.
- Russet, Bruce, International Regions and International Systems, Chicago University Press Chicago, 1967.
- Shahi, Agha, Pakistan Security and Foreign Policy, Progressive Publishers Lahore, 1988.
- Schelling, Thomas, Arms and Influence, Yale University Press, New Haven, 1966.
- Seshgiri, N., The Bomb: Fallout of India's Nuclear Explosion, Delhi, 1975.
- Sherwani, Latif Ahmad, Foreign Policy of Pakistan, Karachi, 1964.

- Sherwani, Latif Ahmad, Pakistan, India and China, Council for Foreign Studies, Karachi, 1967.
- Siddiqui, Aslam, Pakistan Seeks Security, Longman, Lahore, 1960.
- Simpson, John, ed., Nulcear Non-Proliferation: Agenda for the 1990s, New York 1987.
- Singh, Hari, Jai, Kashmir: A Tale of Shame, UBSPD, New Delhi, 1996.
- Singh, Jasjit, India and Pakistan: Crisis of Relationship, Lancer, New Delhi, 1990.
- Singh, Patwant, India and Future of Asia, Alfred A. Knopf, New York 1966.
- Singh, Sampooran, India and Nuclear Bomb, Ministry of Defence Govt. of India, Delhi, 1970.
- Spector, Leonard, Nuclear Proliferation Today, Ventage Books, New York 1984.
- Spector, Lenard S., The Undeclared Bomb: The Spread of Nuclear Weapons 1987-88 Mass, Cambridge, 1988.
- Stanley, John and Pearton, Maurice, The International Trade in Arms, London, 1972.
- Subrahmanyam, K., Indian and the nuclear Challenge, Lancer International, New Delhi, 1986.
- Subrahmanyam, K., Indian Security Perspective, New Delhi, 1982.
- Subrahmanyam, K., ed., Nuclear Myths and Realities A.B.C. Publishing House, N. Delhi, 1981.
- Syed, Anwar H., China and Pakistan: Diplomacy of Entente Cordiale, University of Massachusetts Boston, 1974.
- Thomas Raju, ed., Perspective on Kashmir: The Roots of Conflict in South Asia, west view, boulder, 1992.
- Tickner, J.Ann, Self Reliance Versus Power Politics: The American and Indian Experience in Building Nation States Columbia University Press, Columbia, 1989.
- Trager, F.N. and Krosenberg, P.S., eds. National Security and American Society, University Press of Kansas Lawerence, 1973.
- Vats Bhagat, Foreign Intrigue Against India, New Delhi, 1967.
- Venkataramani, M.S. The American Role in Pakistan, 1947-58, New Delhi, 1982.
- Wander and Arnell, The Proliferation of Advanced Weaponry: Technology, Motivations and Responses Washington, 1992.

- Ziring, Lawerence ed., The Subcontinent in World Politics: India, its Neighbours and the Great Powers Praeger, New York, 1978.

(ii) Articles

- Abid Hussain "India-US Relations" Seminar No.413, January 1994, Page. 34-36.
- Ahmad, Nasir, "The Atomic Energy Commission", Pakistan Quarterly, Vol. X, No.3, Autumn 1957.
- Alam, Aftab, "Brown Amendment and India's Security", Third Concept, Vol.10, No. 115 September 1996.
- Alam, Aftab, "US Military Aid Diplomacy: An Overview", Indian Journal of Politics, Vol. XXIX, Nos. 3-4, 1995.
- Alam, Aftab, "US Post-Cold War South Asian Policy: Opportunities and Challenges", Indian Journal of Politics Vol. XXX, Nos. 1-2, 1996.
- Art, Robert J. "American Foreign Policy and the Fungibility of Force", Security Studies 5(4), Summer 1996.
- Arif, K.M., "Military Balance and National Security", Defence Journal, June 1989.
- Badar Alam Iqbal, "Are Indo-US Economic Relations Really Improving" India Quarterly 51(1) January-March, 1995.
- Barnds, William J., "United States Policy Towards South Asia shifting Perceptions and Policy Choices", Pacific Community, Vol. 3, No.4, July 1977.
- Bhargava, G.S., "Revising US-Pak Military Ties", Hindustan Times, October 27, 1995.
- Bhaskar, C. Uday, "Indian Response to Pakistani Threat", The Times of India, September 10, 1994.
- Burki, S.J. "High Tension and Nuclear Laboratory", Pakistan Quarterly, Vol. X, No.2 Autumn, 1960.
- Cantori, J.J. and Spiegel, S.I., "International Regions: A Comparative Approach to Five Subordinate Systems", International Studies Quarterly, Vol. 13, No.4, December 1969.
- Chakravarthy, Nikhil, "South Asia as a Concept", World Focus, November-December, 1983.
- Cohen, Stephen P., "Is There a Road to Peace in South Asia? An American Perspectives", USI Journal, April-June, 1993.
- Conflicting 'Strategic Interests of the United States and India Evaluating US Army supply to Pakistan", International Studies 29(3) July-September, 1992.

- Dutta, Savita, "US and Indian Non-proliferation Objectives and Concerns", Indian Defence Review, Vol. 9 (3), July 1994.
- Davis, Elizabeth Vanwie and others Structuring an (US) Asian Pacific foreign policy. Journal of Contemporary Asia 26(3) 1996.
- Dhanjal, Gurusharan S., "Ruinous Arms Race", The Hindustan Times, April 27, 1994.
- Dixit, J.N., "US Aid to Pakistan: Continuing an Old Policy ", Indian Express, October 3, 1995.
- Dixit, J.N. India and U.S. in changing world. Mainstream 31(22), 10 April, 1993.
- Dube, Siddarth, US foreign policy after the cold war. Economic and Political Weekly 27(28) 1992.
- Dunn, Lewis, "Containing Nuclear Proliferation", Adelphi Paper, No. 263, Winter 1991.
- Frankel, Benjamin, "The Brooding Shadow: Systematic Imperatives and Nuclear Weapons Proliferation", Security Studies, Nos. 3-4, Spring/Summer, 1993.
- Frankel, Francine R. Indo-US relations: The future is now. Washington Quarterly 19(4) Autumn 1996.
- Ganguly, Sumit, "Avoiding a War in Kashmir", Foreign Affairs, Winter 1990-1991.
- Ganguly, Sumit and Bajpai, Kanti, "India and the Crisis in Kashmir", Asian Survey, Vo. XXXIV, No. 5, May 1994.
- Ganguly, Sumit, "South Asia after the Cold War", The Washington Quarterly, Autumn, 1992.
- Gann, N. Hopes and realities in Indo-U.S. relations: From Cold war to a post-cold war perspective. India Quarterly 48(94) October-December 1992.
- Goldschimdt, Bertrand, "A Historical Survey of Non-proliferation Policies", International Security, Vol.2, No.1, Summer, 1977.
- Gould, Harold A, "Clinton's Moribund South Asian Policy, "The grimes of India, April 20, 1996.
- Gujral, I.K., "Dealing with Washington", The Hindustan grimes, November 7, 1993.
- Haass, Richard N., "USA and South Asia", Strategic Digest, Vol. XX, No.4, April 1990.
- Hames, Tim Foreign policy and the 104th (US) Congress. International Relations 13(1) April 1996.

- Hardgrave, Robert L., "Why India Matters: A Challenge to American Policy in South Asia", Asian Affairs, vol., 11, No.1 Spring, 1934.
- Harrison, Selig S., "India, Pakistan and the USA: Case History of A Mistake, "The New Republic, Vol.141, Nos. 6-7, August 21, 1956.
- Harrison, Selig S., "South Asia and the United States: A Chance for a Fresh Start", Current History, Vol.91, No. No. 563, March, 1992.
- Harrison, Selig S. and others "Indo-American relations". Parlance 16(7-3) April-May 1993.
- Hasan, K. Sarwar, "The Background of American Art Aid to Pakistan", Pakistan Horizon, Vol. XX, No. 2, Second Quarter, 1967.
- Hibbs, Mark; "Dhruva Operating Smoothly". Nucleonics Week, March 26, 1992.
- Hollen, Christopher Van, "The Tilt Policy Revisited: Nixon Kissinger Geopolitics in South Asia", Asian Survey; April, 1980.
- Hussain, Mushahid, "Kashmir Issue: The International Dimension", Parlance, October 1991.
- Indurthy, Rathnam, "The recurring Kashmir crisis since 1947" and its relevance to Indo-American relations in the Bush-Clinton years: An evaluation. Asian Profile 24(3) June 1996 Page 24(3) June 1996.
- Jeevan Kumar, D. Indo-US relations in the nineties new possibilities and opportunities. Indian Journal of American Studies 21(1) Winter 1991.
- Jha, Nalini Kant, Promoting human rights: President Clinton's foreign policy: Dilemma in a changing international order. India Quarterly 51(4) October-December 1995.
- Joeck, Neil, "Tacit Bargaining and Stable Proliferation in South Asia", Journal of Strategic Studies, Vo. 13, No. 3, September 1990.
- Kamath, P.M., "The US Role in South Asia since the end of cold war form partisan to balancer", Strategic Analysis, Vol. XVI, No.9, December, 1993.
- Kamath, P.M., "The Viable Alternative", The Illustrated Weekly of India", April 11-17, 1992.
- Kamath, P.M. The end of the cold war: Implication for India American relations. India Quarterly 49(1-2) January-June 1993.
- Kapila, V., "US Policy in South Asia and its Impact", Indian Defence Review, Vol.9 No.1, January, 1994.

- Kapur, Ashok, "Asia-Pacific: Towards development of bargaining relations between great and minor powers in the 1990s". The Round Table No.340 October 1996.
- Katyal, K.K, "US Expert Moots Partition of J & K", The Hindu, May 7, 1993.
- Kaililzad Zalmay, "Strategic Significance of South Asia" Current History, Vol.181. No.475, May 1982.
- Khalil Zad Zalmay, "The United States in South Asia", Current History vol. 88, no-542 Dec. 89.
- Mahapatra, Chintamani, "The US Pressure on Pakistan: Wasim's Mission to Washington Strategic Analysis October, 1991.
- Mahapatra, Chintamani, "New trends in Indo-American relations". Strategic Analysis 17 (12) March 1995.
- Mahmudul Huque Nuclear proliferation in South Asia and U.S. Policy. International Studies 34(1) January-March 1997.
- Malhotra, Inder, "Of human rights and wrongs: U.S. mood and Vienna meet". Times of India 11 June 1993.
- Malhotra, Vinay Kumar, "Emerging scenario of Indo-US economic relations". Political Economy Journal of India 4(3-4) July-December 1995.
- Malott, John R, "US Interests in India and Pakistan". Strategic Digest, Vol. XXIIL No.7, July 1993.
- Menon, Krishna, "Foreign Policy Continuum", Seminar, November 1965.
- Muni, S.D., "Pak Factor in Indo-US Relations", Mainstream, February 21, 1987.
- Murarka, Dev, "Afghanistan: The Russian Intervention", The Round Table, No. 282, April 1981.
- Nautiyal, Annapurna, "India, Pakistan and the United States in the post cold war era". Asian Studies 15 (1) January-June 1997.
- Naqvi, M.B., "Much Ado about Sale of Junk", The Times of India, October 29, 1995.
- Neier, Aryeh, "The new (US) double standard. Foreign Policy", No.105 Winter 1996-97.
- Neuchterlein, Donald E., "The Concept of National Interest: A Time for New Approach", Orbis, Vol.23, No.1, Spring 1973.
- Panda, Snehalata 'Indo-US relations': "US perceptions, emerging trends in the post cold war period". Foreign Affairs Report 42 (10) October 1993.

- Pandit, K.N., "The American Hand", The Pioneer, November 27, 1993.
- Parischa, S.M., "India's Current Strategic Environment". Strategic Analysis Vol. VIII, August 1984.
- Perkovich, George, "A nuclear Third Way in South Asia", Foreign Policy, Summer 1993.
- Perkovich, George, India, Pakistan and the United States. World Policy Journal 13 (2) Summer 1996.
- Rana, A.P. "Governance by proxy in international relations": The stability problematic and the Pax Delegate in US Foreign policy strategy towards Indian after the cold war. Indian Journal of American Studies 21(1) Winter 1991.
- Rizvi, Nilofar "US foreign policy": A democratic agenda? Mainstream 31(52) 6 November 1993.
- Raphal, Robin, "American and South Asia", Span. Vol. XXXIV, No. 11, November 1993.
- Rao, P.V.R. Chandraslkhar, "Proliferation and the Indian Test: A view from India", Survival, Vol. XVI, No. 5, September-October, 1974.
- Rasgotra, Maharaj Krishna, "America Meddles in Kashmir again", The Hindustan Times, June 3, 1993.
- Raza Maroof, "The Hang Proposal: No Real Threat to India", Financial Express, October 13, 1995.
- Robinson, William I. Globalisation, the world system and 'democracy promotion' in US foreign policy. Theory and Society 25(5) October 1996.
- Rosenthal, A.M., "Kashmir's Far - reaching Impact ", Foreign policy Bulletin, March 1, 1957.
- Rustamji, K.F. "The tilt in American policy", Radical Humanist 57(11) February 1994
- Sathe, R. M., "Pokharan Experiment can be Beginning of a New Era", Yojna, August 1, 1974.
- Schulz John J. "Riding the Nuclear Tiger: The Search for Security in Asia" Arms Control Today, June 1993.
- Shah, Viren J. "India USA relations": A BJP perspective. Organiser 46(2) 14 August 1994,.
- Sharma, Ritu, "India's Autonomy and American Assistance: Politics of uneven Equation", Strategic Analysis, October 1991.

- Shrivastava, B. K., "Indo-American Relation: Search For A- New Equation", International Studies, Vol. 30, No.2, April June 1993.
- Singh, K.R., "Power Without Greatness", Seminar, May 1991.
- Singh Jaswant, "Capping and all that: Non-proliferation, Missiles and Indo-US Relations", Frontline, May-June 1994.
- Singh S. Nihal, "Can the US and India be Real Friends", Asian Survey, September 1983.
- Singh, S.K, "The Ghost of Dulles", The Hindustan Times, November 24, 1995.
- Smith, Gerard C. and Cabban, Helena, "A Blind Eye to Nuclear Proliferation", Foreign Affairs, vol. 68, No.1, Summer 1977.
- Spector, Leonard, "India-Pakistan War: It Could be Nuclear", New York Times, June 7, 1990.
- Subrahmaniyam, K., "Don't Brood Over Brown", The Economic Times, November 1, 1995.
- Subramanayam, R.R., "Indo-US Security Relations" Strategic Analysis, May 1991.
- Subrahmanyam, K. "India and U.S.: A long tango". Economic Times 8 September 1993.
- Subrahmanyam, K. Indo-U.S. relations: Pealing with Bill Clinton. Economic Times 28 January 1993.
- Tanham, George, "Indian Strategic Culture", Washington Quarterly, Winter 1992.
- Thakur, Ramesh, "India and the United States": A triumph of hope over experience. Asian Survey 36(6) June 1996.
- Thakur, Ramesh Chandra, "India After Non-Alignment", Foreign Affairs, Spring 1992.
- Thomas Raju, G.C. "Prospects for Indo-US Security Ties", Orbise, Summer 1983.
- Thomas Raju, G.C., "Strategic Relationship in Southern Asia Differences in Indian and American Perspective", Asian Survey, July 1981.
- Thornton, Thomas Perry, "Between the Stools: US Policy towards Pakistan During Carter Administration", Asian Survey, October 1982.
- Thornton, Thomas Perry, The New Phase in US- Pakistani Relations", Foreign Affairs Vol. 68, No.3, Summer, 1989.

- Travis, Tom A., "Indo-American Relations: The Kashmir Controversy", India Quarterly, Vol. XLIX, No.4, October-December 1993.
- US defers action against India under super 301. Economic Times 15 June 1990.
- The U.S. India trade relationship: Economic Studies 36(4) 16 August 1997.
- Venkataramani, M.S. and Arya, H.C., "American's Military alliance with Pakistan: The Evolution and course of an uneasy relationship", International Studies, vol.3, Nos. 1-2, July-October 1996.
- Venkateswaran, A. P. "New Paradigms in Indo-US Relations", World Focus, Nov.-Dec. 1991.
- Vinod, M. J., "Attitude Towards India: Contrasting Approach of the United States and the Soviet Union", India Quarterly, Vol.46. No.1, Jan-Mar. 1990.
- Vinod, M. J., Clinton Administration and Indo-US Ties", Mainstream, Vol.31, No.11 January 1993.
- Vohra, A. M. "Ban Nuclear Arms", The Hindustan Times, December 10, 1993.
- Vora, Batuk; New U.S. outburst on Kashmir: Clinton's bumbling foreign policy. Mainstream (Annual Number) 20 November 1993.
- Wisner, Frank G. Indo-American partnership: An investment in the future. Economic Studies 30(s), Spring 1995.
- Wirsing Robert G. and Roherty, James M., "The United States and Pakistan", International Affairs autumn 1982.
- Zuberi, M., "India in the Nuclear Age", USI Journal, Vol. CXXIII, No. 514, Oct-Dec. 1993.
- Zutshi, Amar, " India's Peace Bomb", Statesman, April 25, 1990.
- Zutshi, Amar, "Indo-US Military Tie-up", Mainstream, Vol.30 No.7 December 1991.

Index

❑ ❑ ❑

Notes

Notes